AF587474

SHE WILL LAST AS LONG AS STONES

SHE WILL LAST AS LONG AS STONES

kathy wu

Wendy's Subway

For Ma (1963–2023), for everything.

Let us never forget: that the poem was entombed in a collapse of the earth. By habit, rather than commodity, the singularity and multiplicity of things were presented as divided couples and dualities, before the genres and species were discovered. This cadence allowed for a better distinction between things. . . . But we're also waiting for the renewed perception of differences to reveal themselves as such, and for the poem to reemerge once more.

— Édouard Glissant, *Poetics of Relation*

GROUND

土

EARTH

Chuquicamata———Codelco———Antofagasta, Chile———-22.289, -68.900

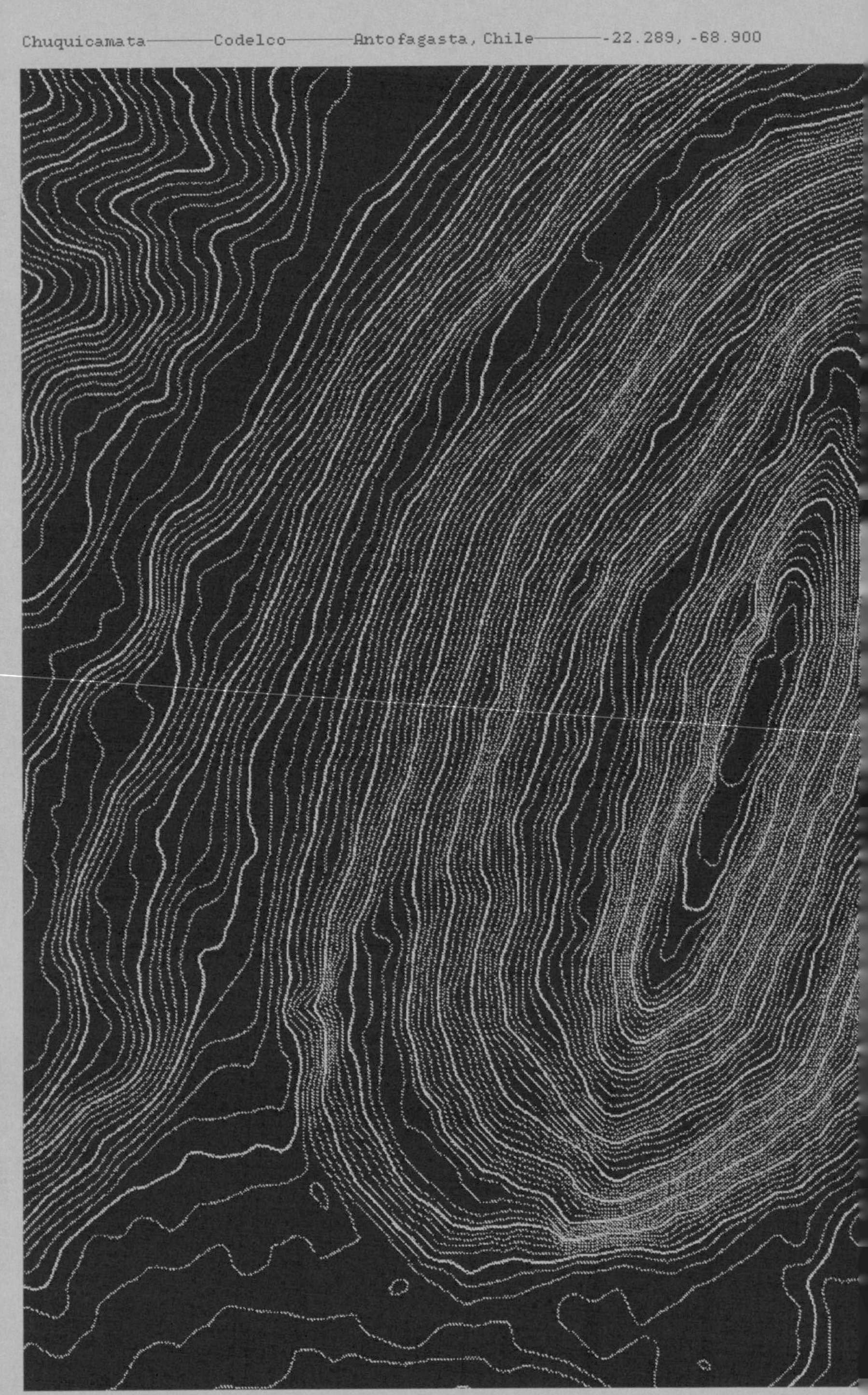

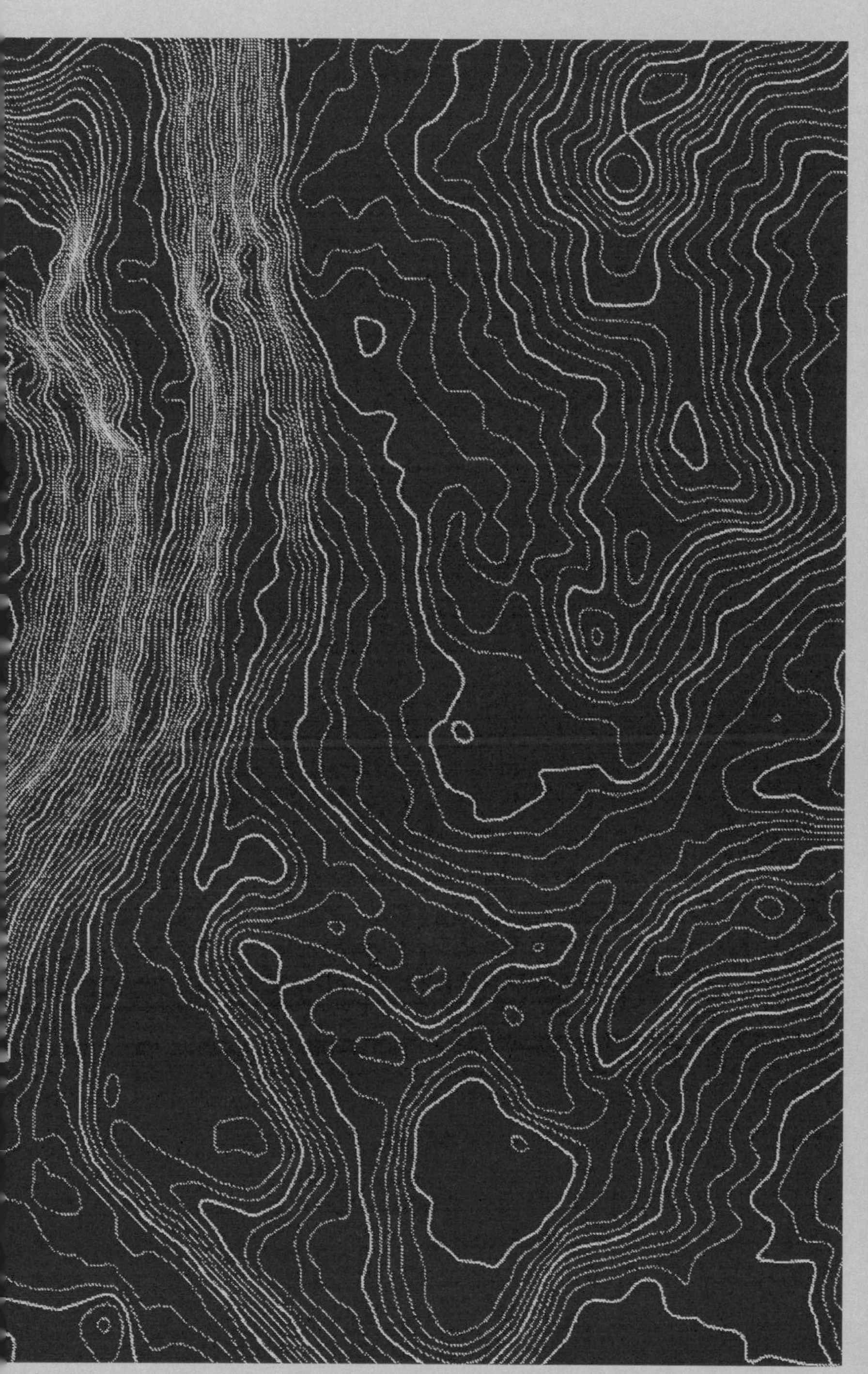

Cerro Verde——Freeport McMoRan——Arequipa, Peru——-16.531, -71.604

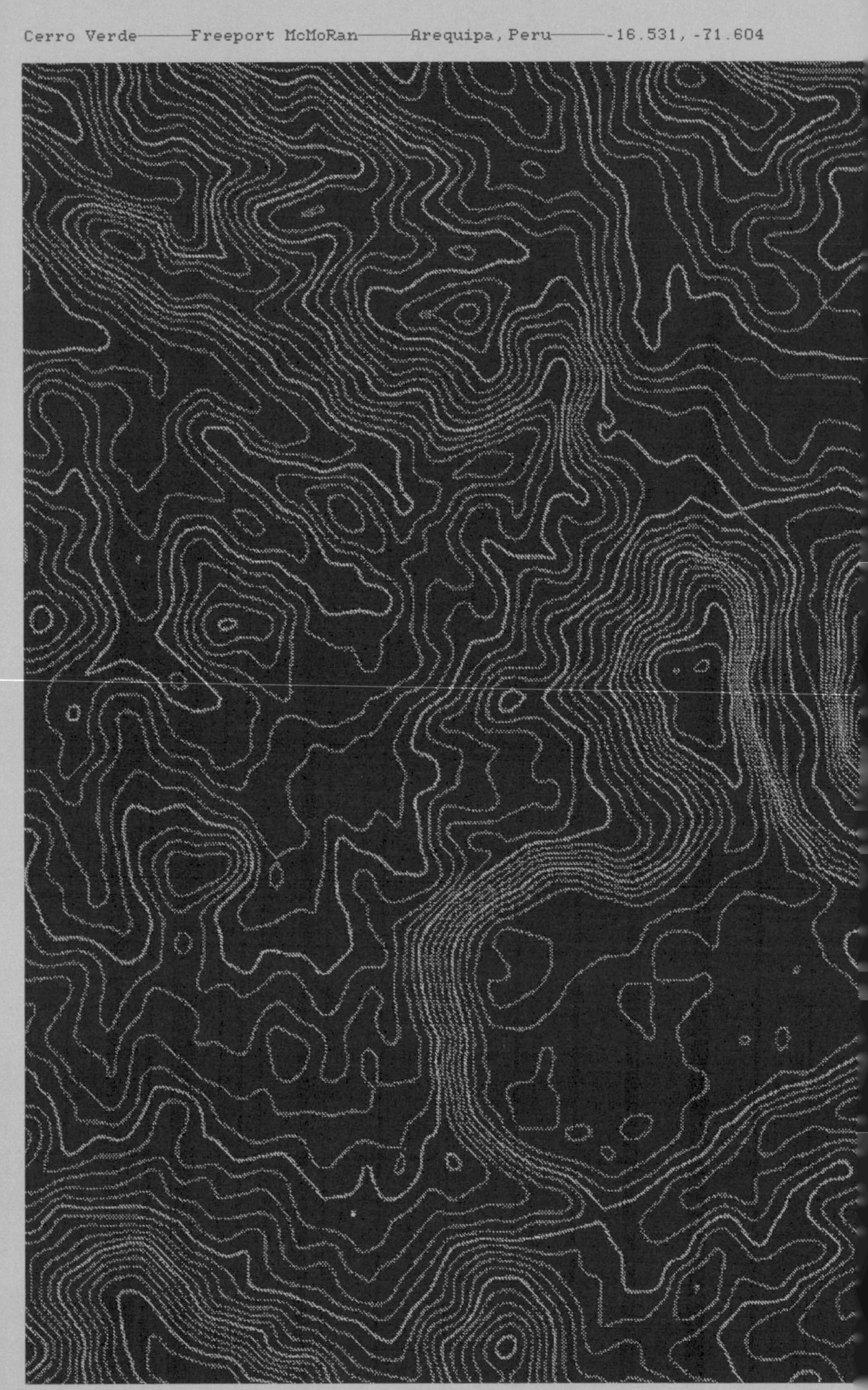

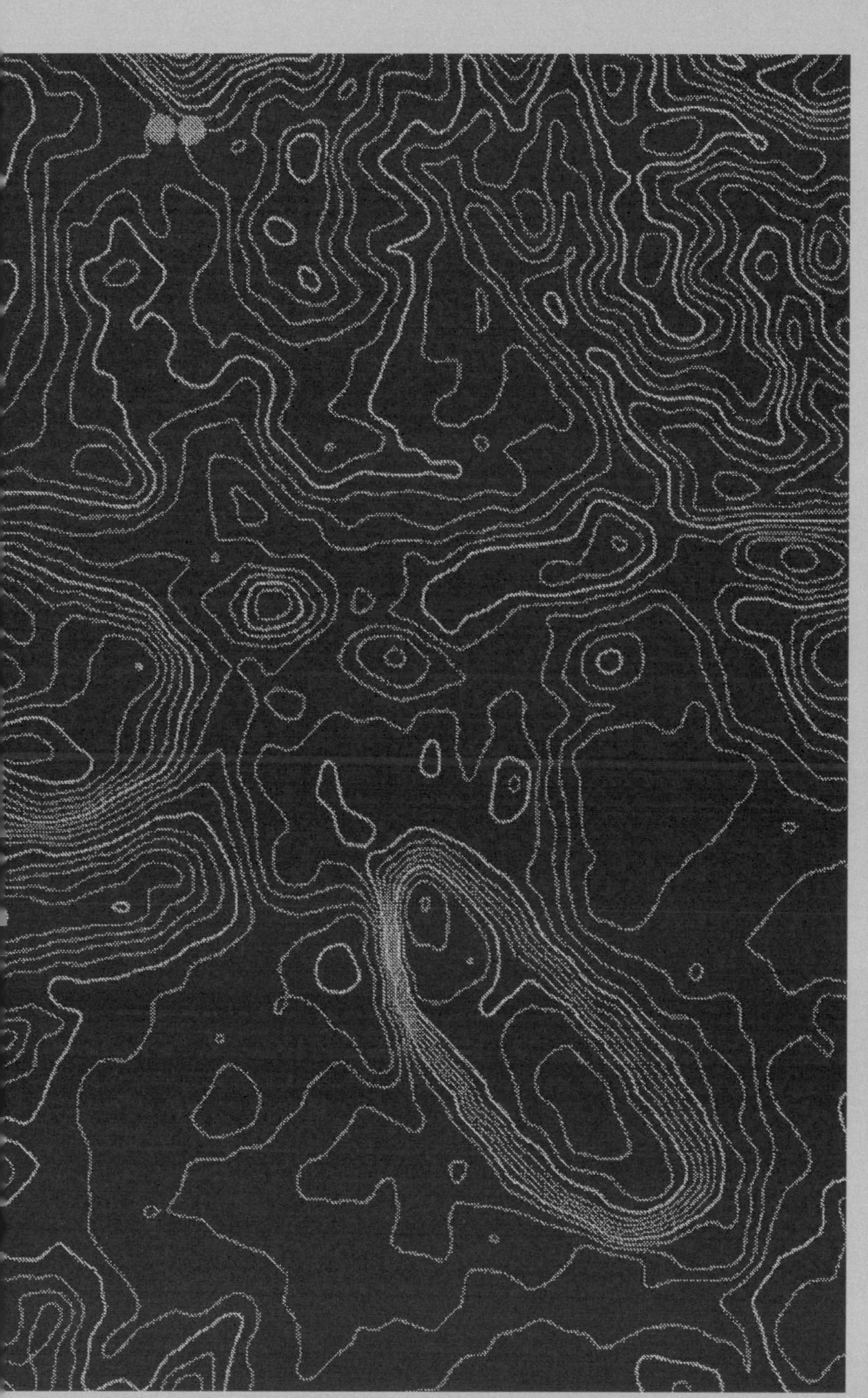

卌 : OCEAN

Name every place that used to be ocean.

DOES IT BECOME DESERT

I thought the stones would answer, as if grief was a question. Ammonite along arm's length, abundance, angiosperms, each one of you is a glyphic thing, inscribing a geo-love—a lithic history. How long. Sunday at midnight is when people appear / the pink-white crescent of your fingernail. You can offer it language; the color is all but micaceous. Early theories of stone precipitated (neptunic). Perhaps water houses such things: granite, schist, basalt.

Hot dust, cold dust, congeals fast. In the beginning, fusion forms entire gods: nuclear heat. Faster + faster, twirls in her silver-gold skirt. Shades of yellow, red, to shield your eyes from. Metals precipitate from sun, iron to gooey center. Everything slows, dries, crisps the surface.

Become blue-green. Become submerged in so much rain. Algae blooming + dying. The syntax of cells warps at incredible speed. Wet + breathing things. The first thing to blink at light. Plates crash, pull at dermis. Violent, slow orogenies. The migration of very large animals eventually. What invitation (asteroid). How many elegies held in sediment by now? Cambrian soft life, press jelly craters to sand / undulations where water used to be. Geology as a thing to be read. Everything has to return to the ground. This is a gray-brown truth. There are so many mothers in the fossil record. There are so many bellies.

THE DESERT SAYS

The sun takes seven minutes to reach. It is taking a while. It is forgetful. Sand is. Wind is. Wind never forgets. Water doesn't. Be born here. Nothing has changed. The cacti gloaming. The sand yellow-brown. Be underwater, a billion years ago. Copper underground here. Nuggets gleam (turquoise). Erect a saguaro in which a small owl is burrowed. Imprint of an old life. Early weavings of copper in the American Southwest. Where lightning hits sand, fractals emerge / crystallize as thought. Dendrites, white stoichiometric teeth. What odds. What a warm place for a plane to land. Sand is a million tiny words. Sand promises, *The end won't be all that different from the beginning.*

For stone to metastasize it must speak English well.
For stone to metastasize it must have living family
here. For stone to pretend to be orphaned.
That's nonsense. I'm underwater now. Twenty-nine
first Christmases. That's the American dream.
There is no Christmas in the cave house. Grandfather's
Loess Plateau / loss plateau. It is the same color
as Tucson. Iowa's geologic twin. The hard bed
bread-warm from the hearth. A goat in the yard.
No circuitry here. Just red manifestos + a promise.
Don't romanticize: only knew about it after the
funeral. Don't want to talk to anyone on WeChat.
This is the great globalized age we live in.

⏚ : TRACING

Make a tiny shift.
Let trace become fossil.

 of plants and animals———Pleistocene Epoch (2.58 million–11,700

TU

Loess / loose / lose you. Germanic, sure. Yellow, but not gold. So the river goes. Here on the loss plateau, everything is yellow. 土 inverts sky / a double horizon / circuitries of dirt.

It is easy to know the provenance of the loss.

When I was born, the color yellow. This + more was revealed to you (hypnotherapy). The sun maybe the water maybe the emperor maybe the roots maybe the soil—yes, all that + more. That's home. Loamy gold + tendency to erode.

years ago)——Glacial and interglacial cycles with the existence

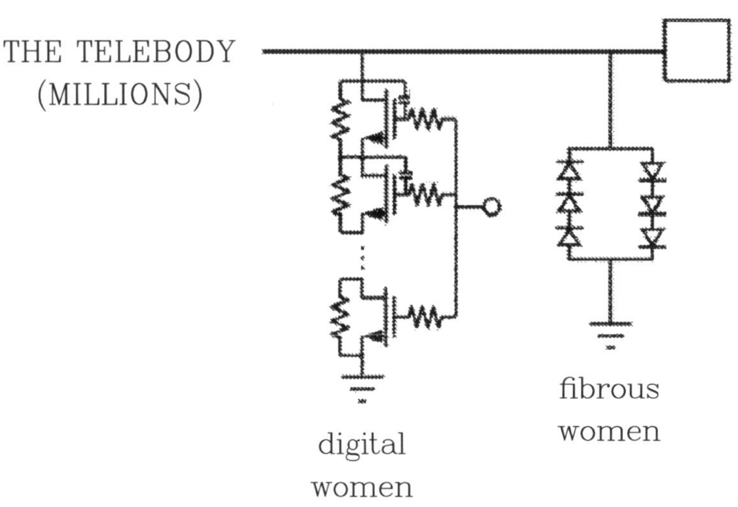

Fig. 1: ESD protection scheme using
anti-parallel diode-string structure

MOTHER-DAUGHTERBOARDS

Deftness crossing articulations. Forgetfulness orbits an infinite spindle. Copper weavings are precursor to motherboards—could you transform the textile of knowing?

Particles pulsing (yellow). Women that distilled logic from warp. What persists after the mass to energy equation? Mother seems infinite: in each cone of light, each wash of green. The word exits the mouth.

Daughterboards. Copper + the dawn of electricity. Paul Revere; Canton, MA; the first electric lamp; the first American copper smelter. The lacemakers (Guggenheims) striking it big—expedition to Chile. GUGGENEX (Google).

It is touching you —/\/\/— through semi-conduction, migrant worker, post-Immigration Act parent, the same village not enough to level us. Unskilled labor cutting out glass, plastic.

Metal is no mother: what remains is data / TXT logs / a JPEG encoded as garble. The first proverb she taught me: endless vistas reward efforts. Live to see the end of the world, the China virus. Marquees ticker.

THE CIRCUITRY BOOM

Mother was a rectangle maker—intricate
weavings of copper, silicon, germanium, rendered
in fine + brown lines. They mesmerize with
their beauty. To know the way of invisible things:
air, electricity, waves.

To know the name of every quantifiable thing.
In absence of sleep, memorize: scientific names
for animals, digits of pi, names of stone.

Deluge of possibility. The Chinese character for stone:
a mouth, the word for *opening* is a near perfect
square, ornamented with the black furniture of legs.
A screen.

FIGURATION

The clock trickles + I am washing you, the long brown lines of your belly, underarms. The water is hot. As I clean you, remember we are made out of mud.

I am putting socks on your feet. Every movement feels backward. The heels always surprise me, detouring bone. The toenails surprise me, growing despite the legs—

⊣|| : LIKENESS

At any phase:
Tell the moon all the ways in which you look alike.

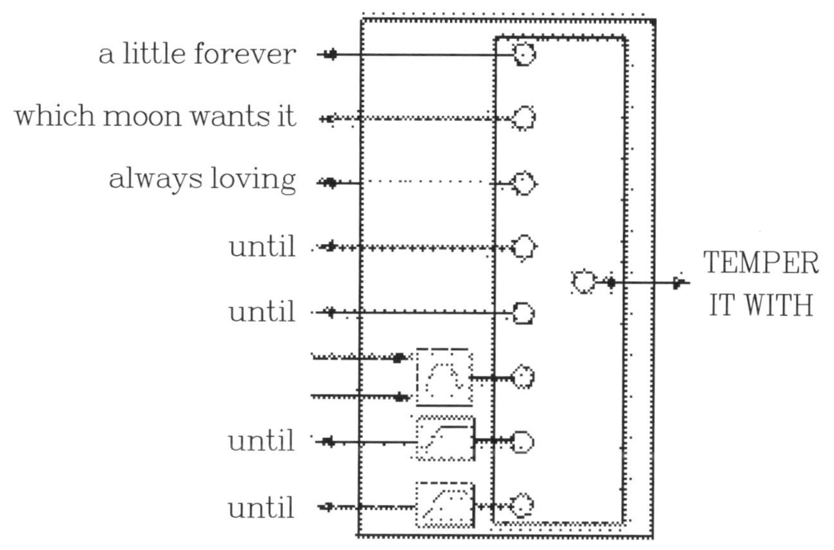

Fig. 2: SP8T RF switch diagram

MNEMONIC (FIGMENT STUDY)

The mother scolds the horse. Does the mother scold? I am learning colors with you. Red, yellow. I try to say what an intimate curl of tongue can't reach yet, something between drop of jade, mouth of water. You say, *green*. I say, *deer*. What also sounds like, *road*. What sounds like, *marination*; *flute*. You laugh. We practice until the sound becomes muscle, becomes closer to the feeling of walking.

MY MEMORY HAS NO HALF-LIFE

We are grown isotopes drifting. I will love you until the heat death of the universe.

Forensic defiance, forest fires abound. California made of five thousand little islands. You know the schtick. Sand + a tenderness. Trace it with —w— your finger. I wanted to change my name, but ancestor grave. Every force meets an equal + opposite, right?

⊣⫴ : SPEECH

Follow a rivulet of water until it becomes the last thing you each said.

PNEUMONIC

A cell is the smallest unit of life, the way that $I + a$
are the smallest in English.

How long does it take to turn inanimate?
How long does it take to jump from lung to rib?
From rib to spine. Will it remember the language
of lung?

Slow moss wrapping greenly around the gray of it.
Eyes that closed before the end of the world.

KNOWLEDGE ISN'T
AT HOME ANYWHERE.

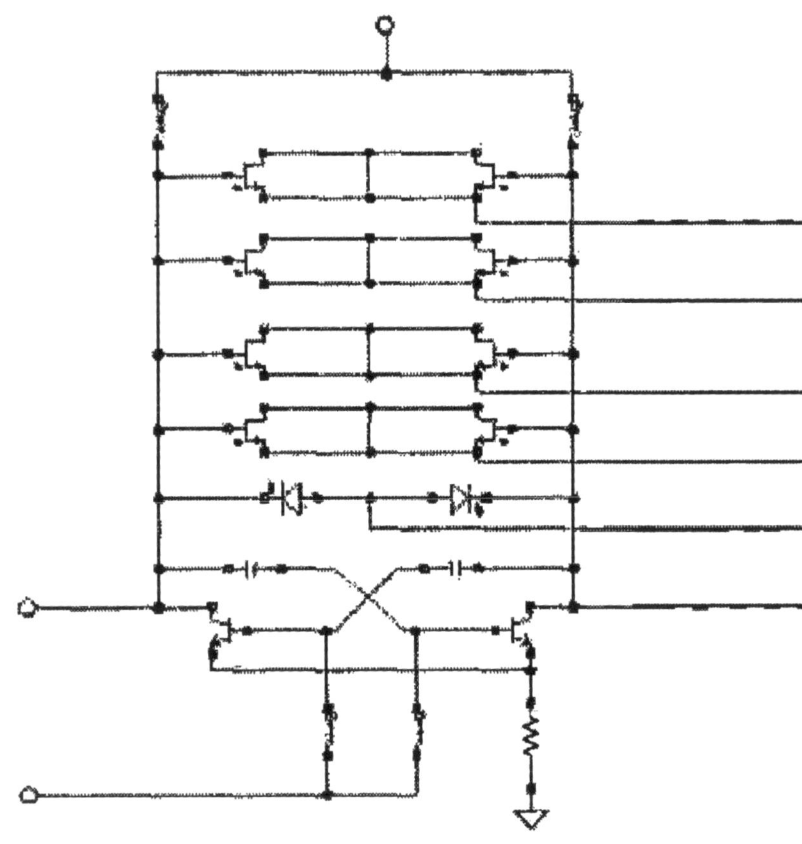

Fig. 3: Schematic of a cross-coupled gate neutralized amplifier

How much energy in the letter *A*.

Meanwhile, pluralities remain.

For, let *I* be zero.

That's the thing about hardware.

For let earth. Earth is earth plus one.

For let stone. Stone is stone minus one.

Forget stone.

MOON / MOM

She will last as long as stones, a tarp of water.
Two frogs + four fish. Ashen shale, agro-industrial
edge. The undead / those glassy forevers.

The ocean flat + still. The planet Mars. Chang-e on
the other side of the moon.

Those explorations, excavations. The old Chinese
proverb. Oh, what a mess you're making. Stratigraphy
through the ages. Wash it down with a little stone.
Half-lives flitting. Earthenware. Where is it. This is
not a Chinese + American poem. I suppose it accrues
sediment. The house I grew up in overgrown
with ferns.

In one dream, a poem is made of vectors of wind.
I am blowing over the Pacific, a bellyful of current.
Leaning into an opacity that I love. I am not sure
where the poem resides. Whether empty / electric.
Fermenting + full of seeds (white). Unsure if
stamina to carry on. Land on the dark side, anyway.

⊣|ı : SWALLOW

At what point do you become sea?
How close might you get without going under?

A FRAGMENTED LINEAR ACCOUNT

Lyell's. No–
contemporary
stratigraphy:
disturbed, illegible,
entangled. Is all
climate writing pastoral
or elegy? You're
tenacious to
think it will last.
War going on.
When list points
to infinity +
elegy to zero,
what do endings
offer? This is an
incomplete gesture.
Endless names of
stones. This
cannot be the ending,
yes? Earthly
goods cannot be
the ending.

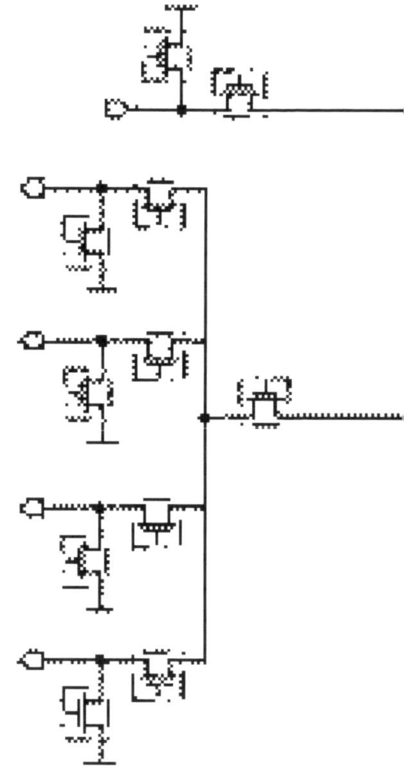

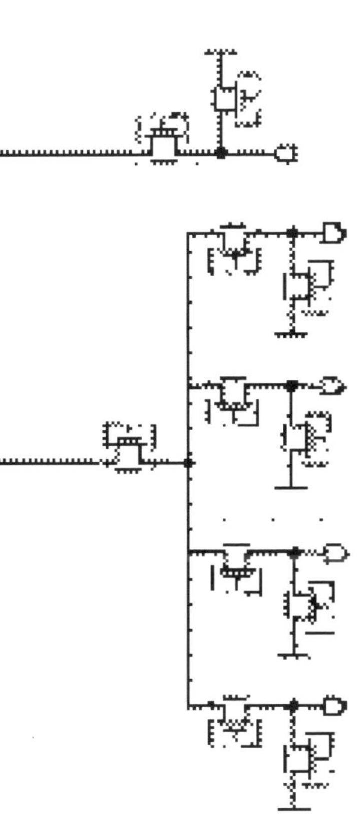

Fig. 4: A simplified SP10T T/R switch topology

Knife, scalpel.
I can't
remember if
dynamite or
what. Salt
peter in the
south, copper
north. Stars
there so you
don't forget.
Graphic chip
there so you
don't forget.
Universe
blackened and
gooey. How
much lithium
do you want,
electric brain.
Pass a law,
why don't
you, Bitcoin
mining keeps.
Protected
interests of
corporations.
They hate
birds.

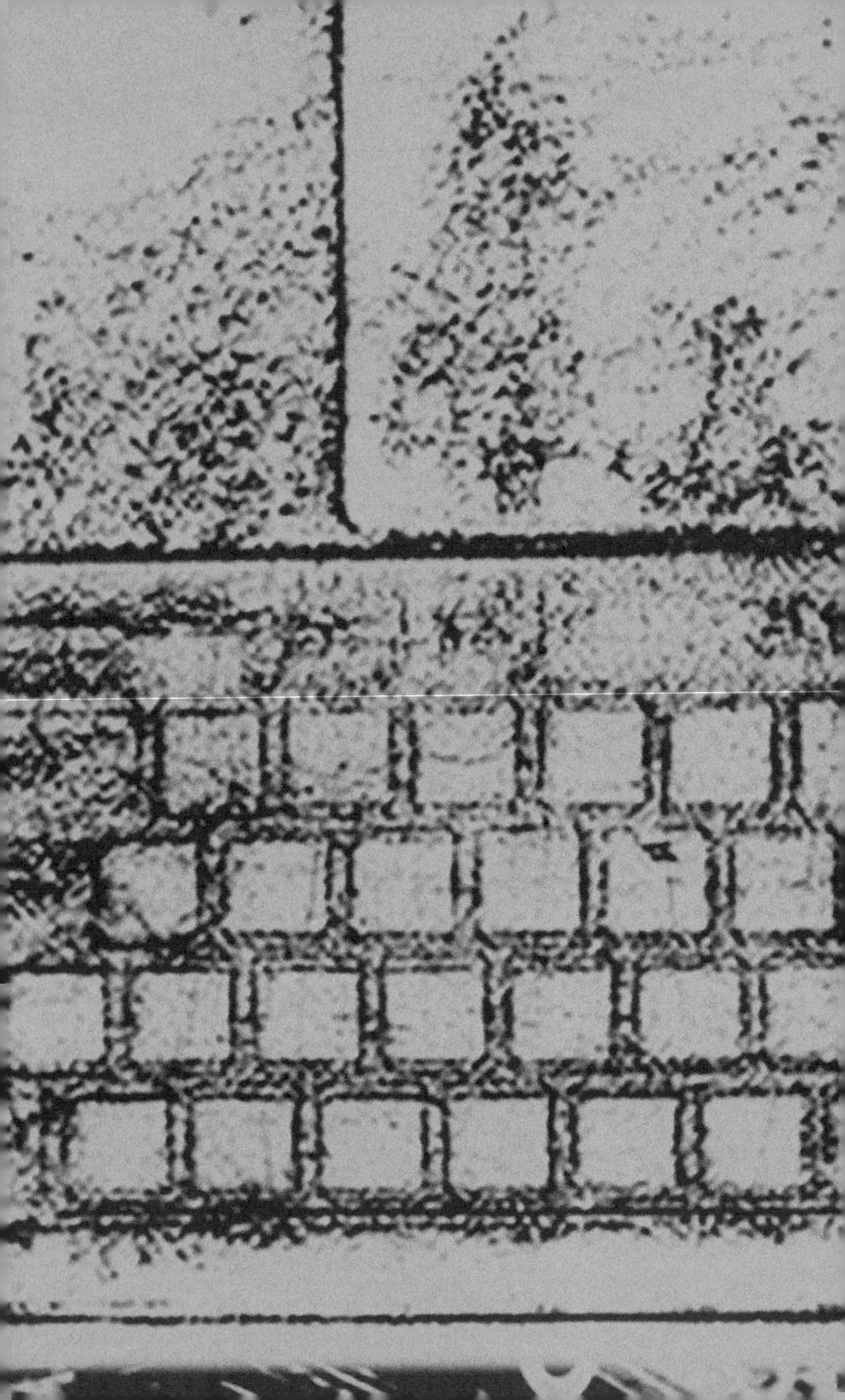

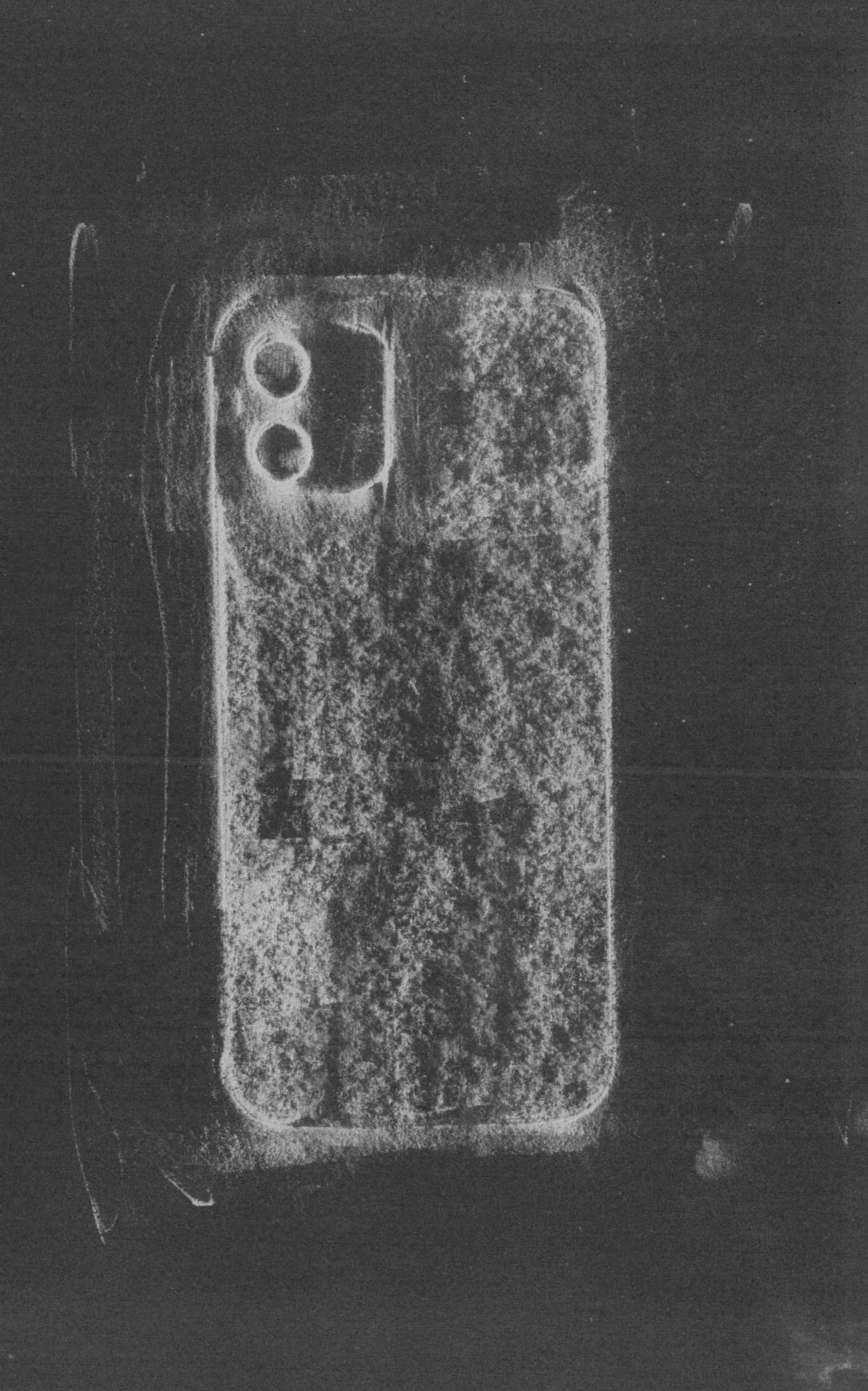

El Teniente——Codelco——Machalí Chile——-34.0878, -70.458

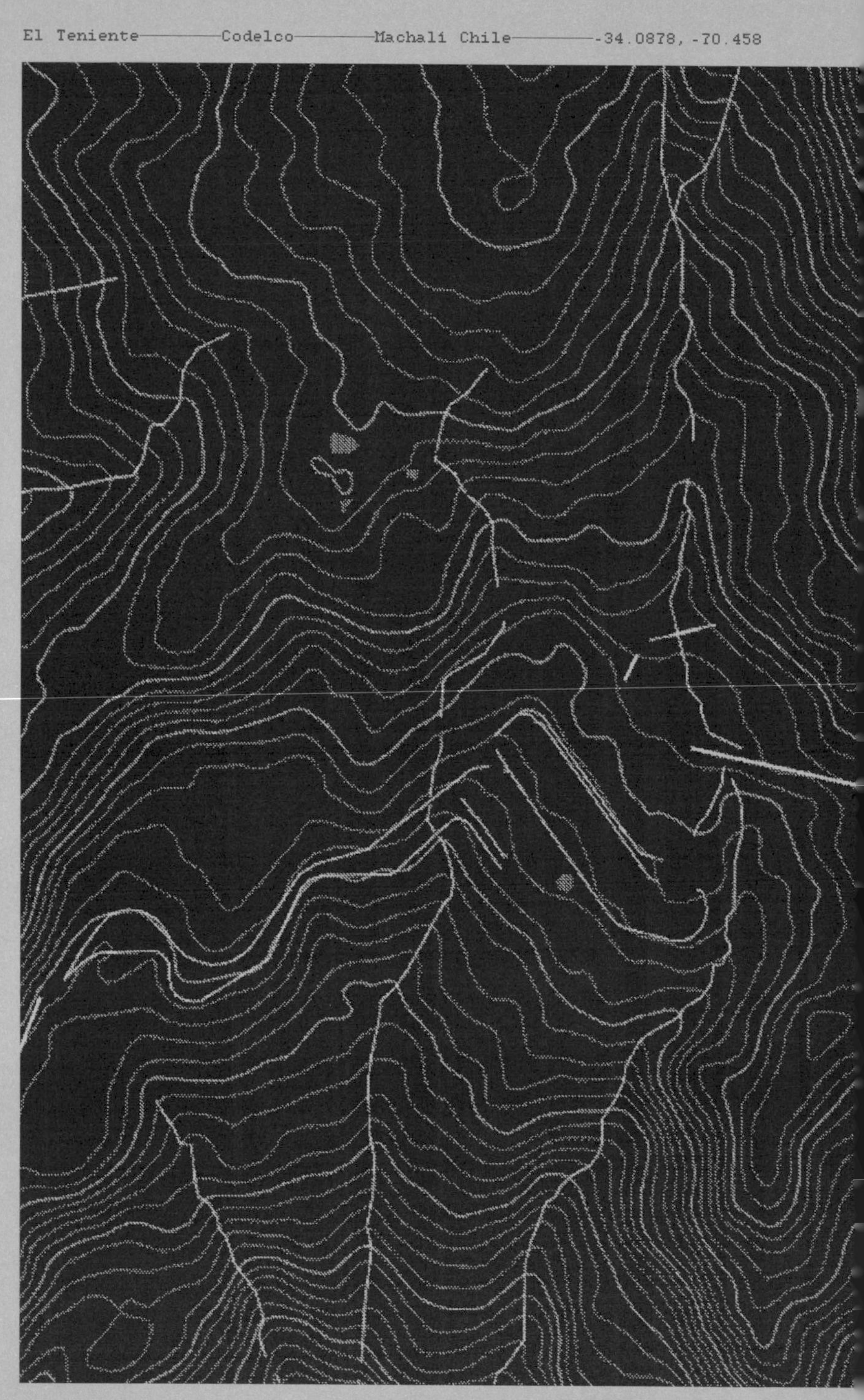

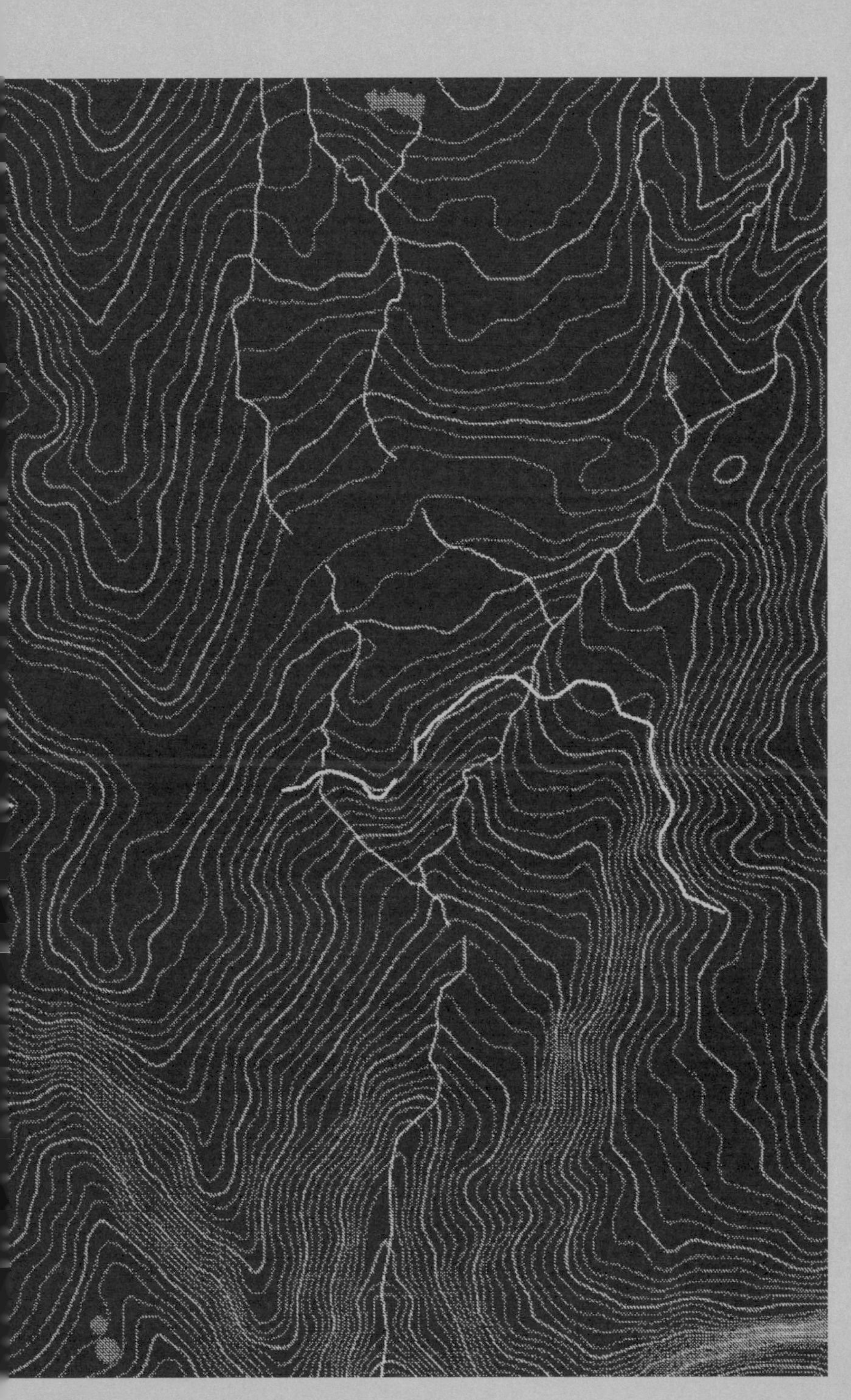

BOOKS OF THE DEAD

The largest mining accident known to man.
Carbon monoxide in a hole. Cup it with your hands.
Everything on fire—

What kind of forensic pain. All I see is graphite.
Pixelography. Not made of language, that's for sure.
Everything brown, orange. Labyrinths (dark).
The skin sheds, but it's an old snake. Red-brown,
orange-brown, dry dust, cement, gray edge,
mud fall, dirt sky, dust leg, stone man, father, son,
granite body—

Some act of faith, don't say hell. Dirt cloud, ore river.
Empire lasts in funny ways. Bowling alley (vestige).
Swimming pool (vestige). This looks like fucking
Mars. Ballroom, social velvet, no plants. All I see is
representation. Stop. Elon is running to catch the
legacy. Don't say lithium-ion battery.

Picture of miner + miner families.
Picture of tunnel with stone at the end of it.
Picture of no plants.
Picture of bus with no workers.
Picture of small precipice.
Picture of no riot.
Picture of no air.
Picture of website.
Picture of word made light.
Picture of number getting smaller + smaller.

CITY OF STAIRS

One percent—I mean, zero point zero zero one percent. The thinning. Pure stuff. Say it's a crisis. Be born here—here. The City of Stairs. Does it compute? Theater posters of Marlon Brando, *George of the Jungle*. Empire lasts in funny ways. Old church color of sky, color of air / local squatters meet God in decay. Color of miner mothers , miner lovers, miner deities; he's got no face. Pareidolia. Plastic flowers. Things under feet include concrete. Include orange Andes. Include copper.

So yes, I would say it's fundamentally a technology of abstraction. I mean extraction. Language is. No, technology is.

Anaconda has shares. GUGGENEX has shares. Bingham has shares, Kennecott has shares. Try to tell the truth. Try so that the poem isn't mud.

Picture of rock Jesus.
Picture of body older than man.
Picture of prospects.
Figure of rig.
Figure of terrace
for workers quarters.
Figure of smelter.
Figure of internet.
Relax. Let the internet move into you.

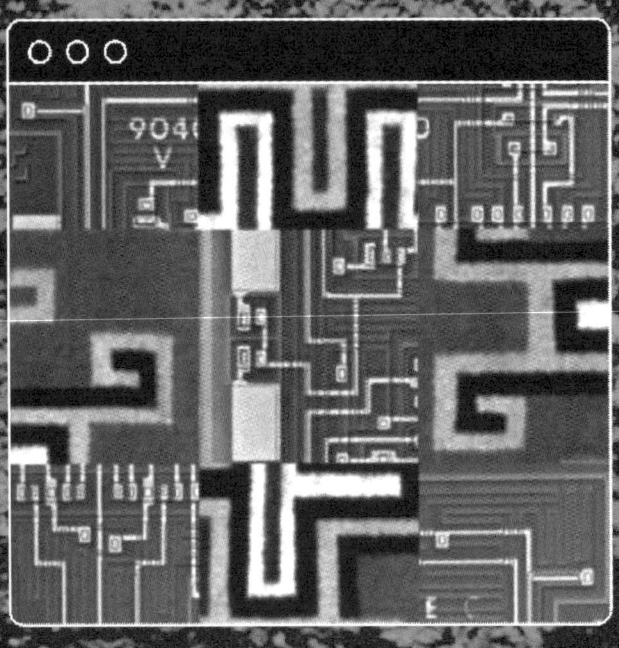

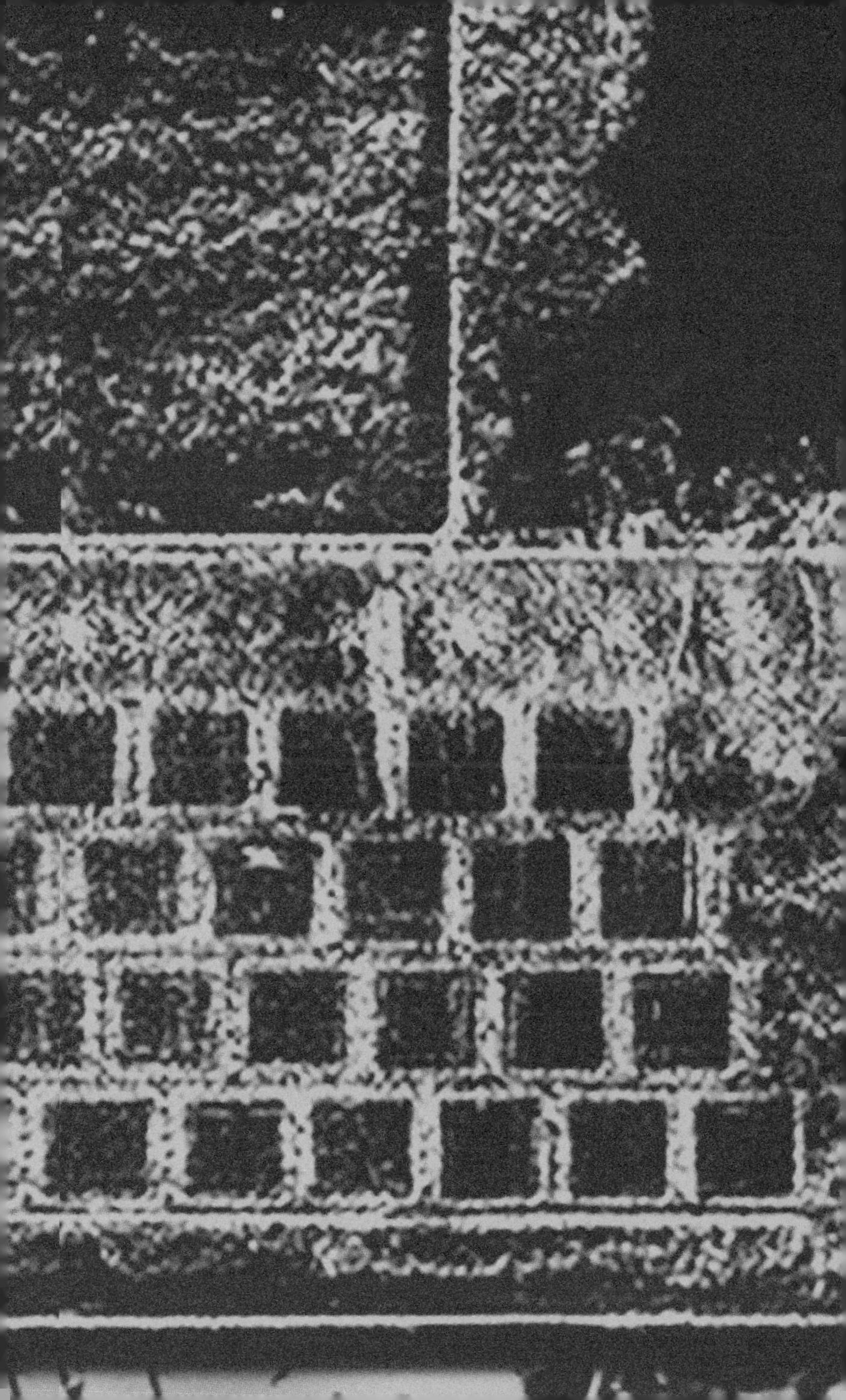

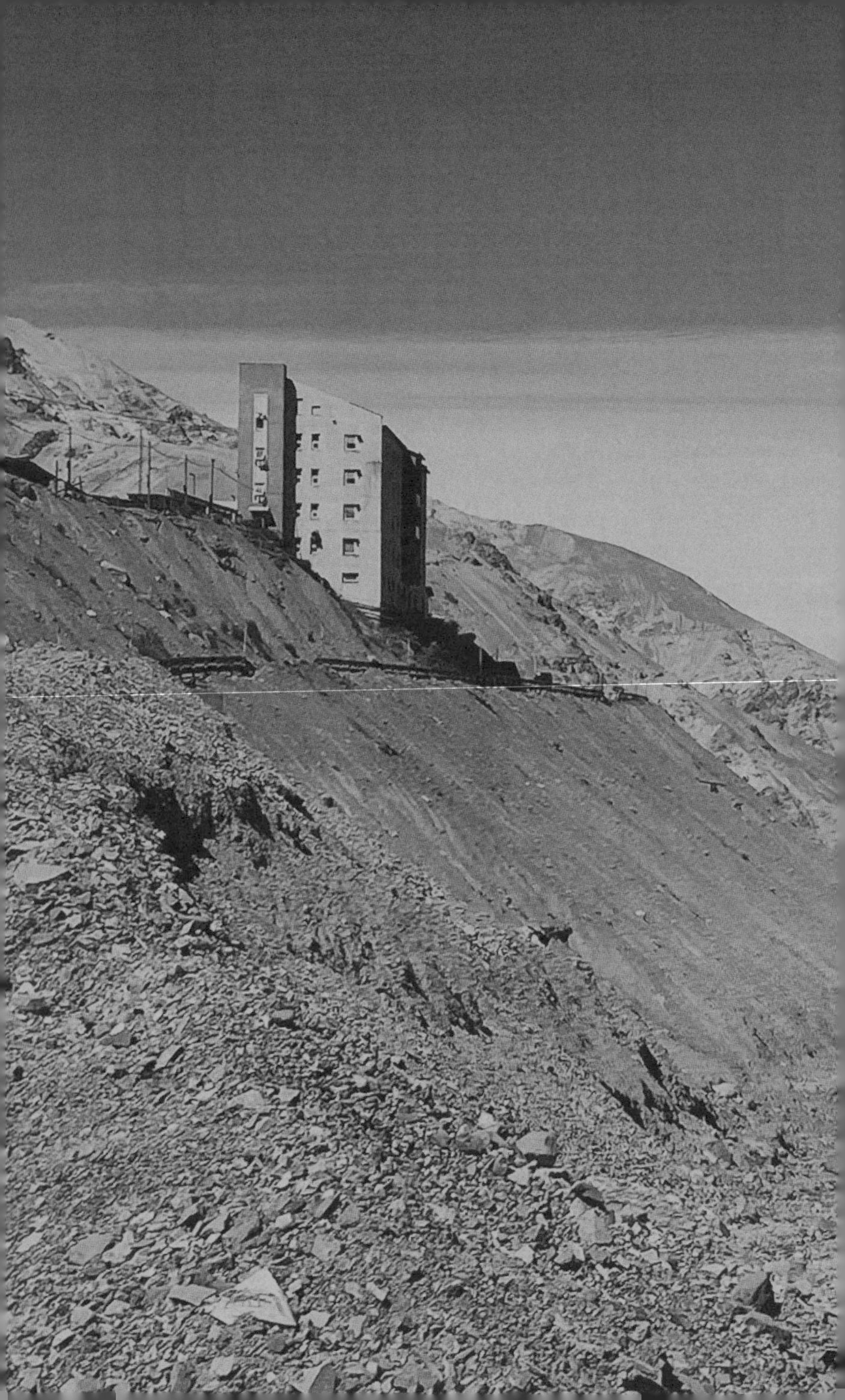

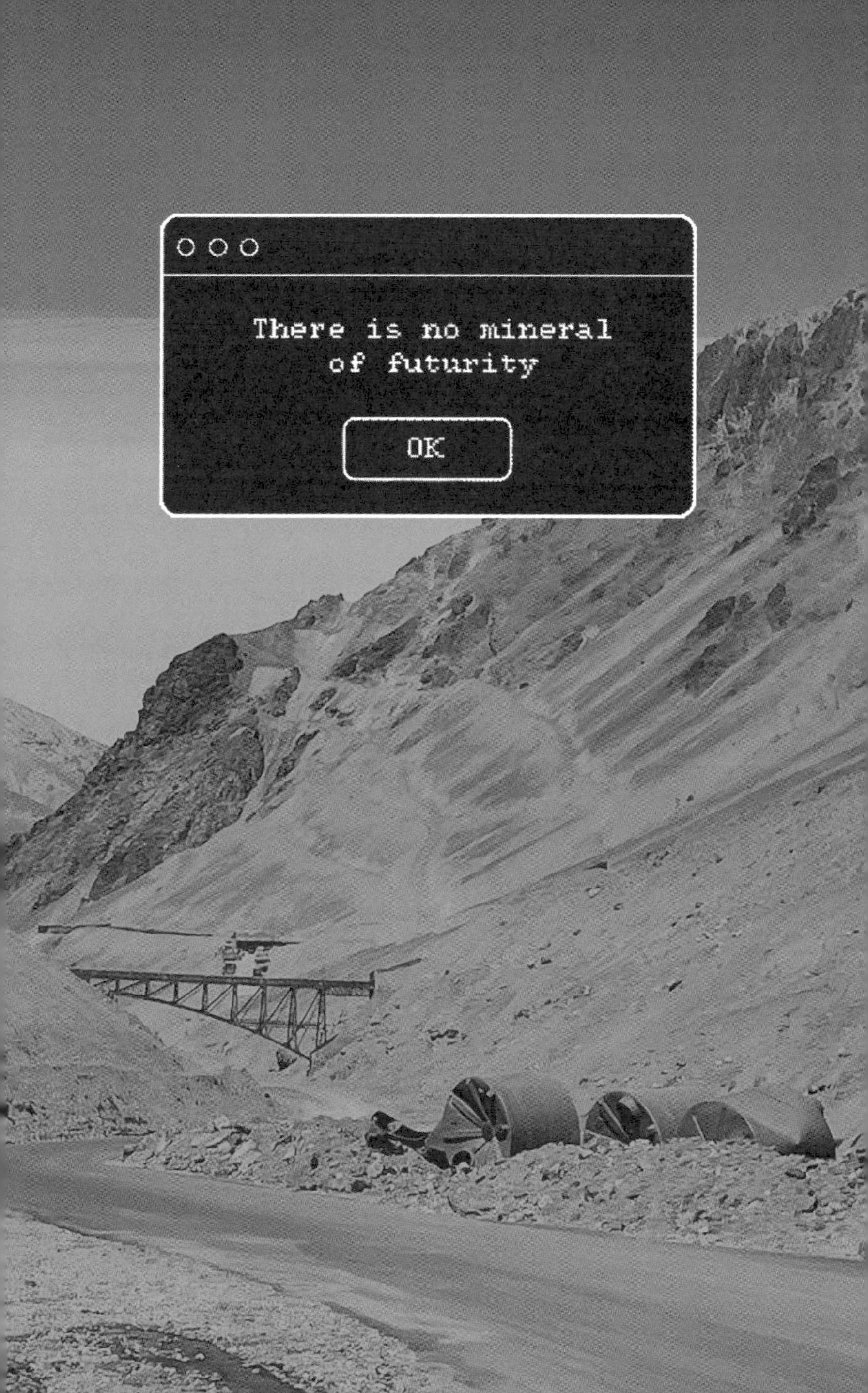
There is no mineral
of futurity
OK

Kamoa-Kakula——Ivanhoe Mines——Muvunda, Congo-Kinshasa——-10.883, 25.198

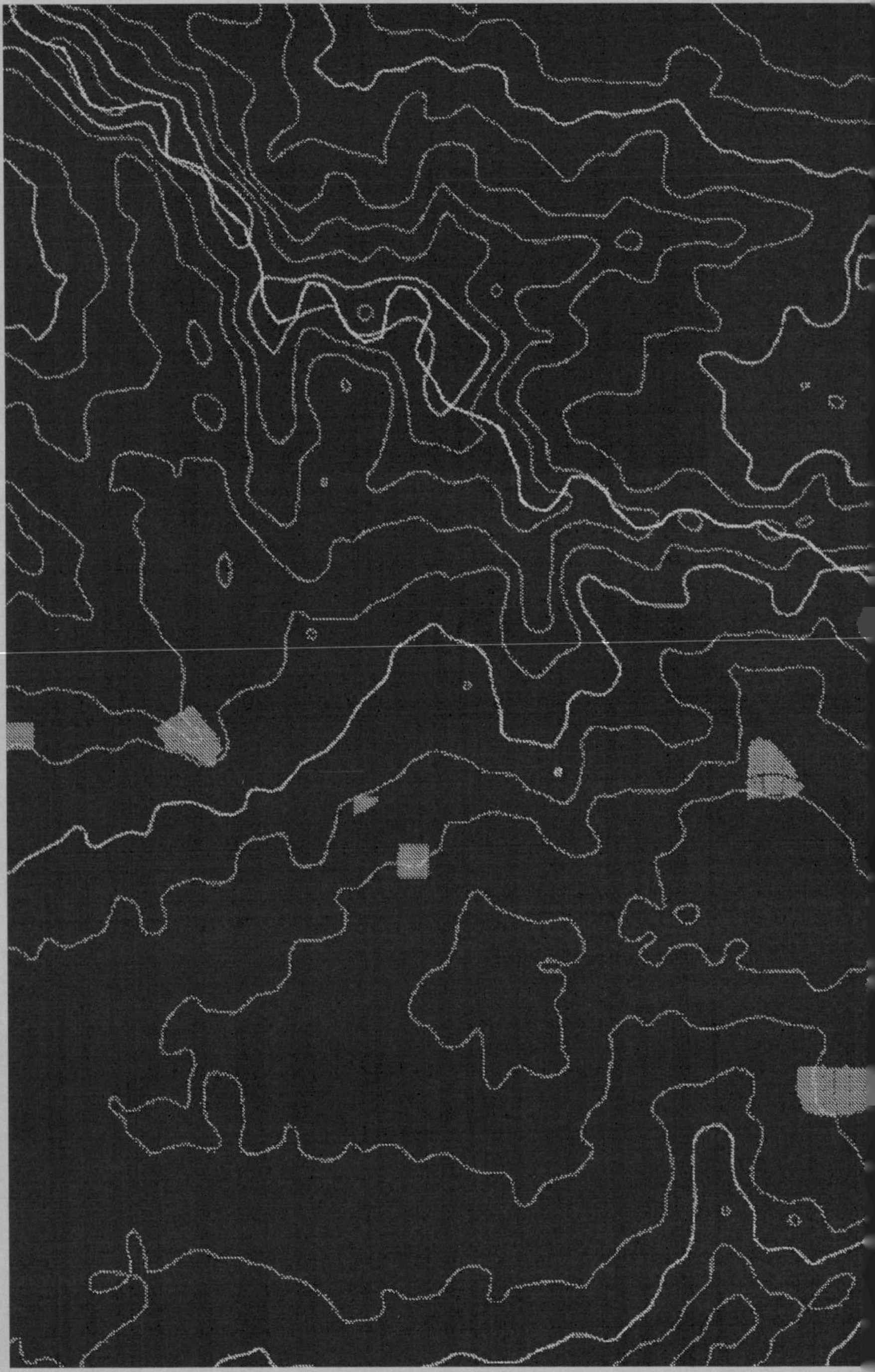

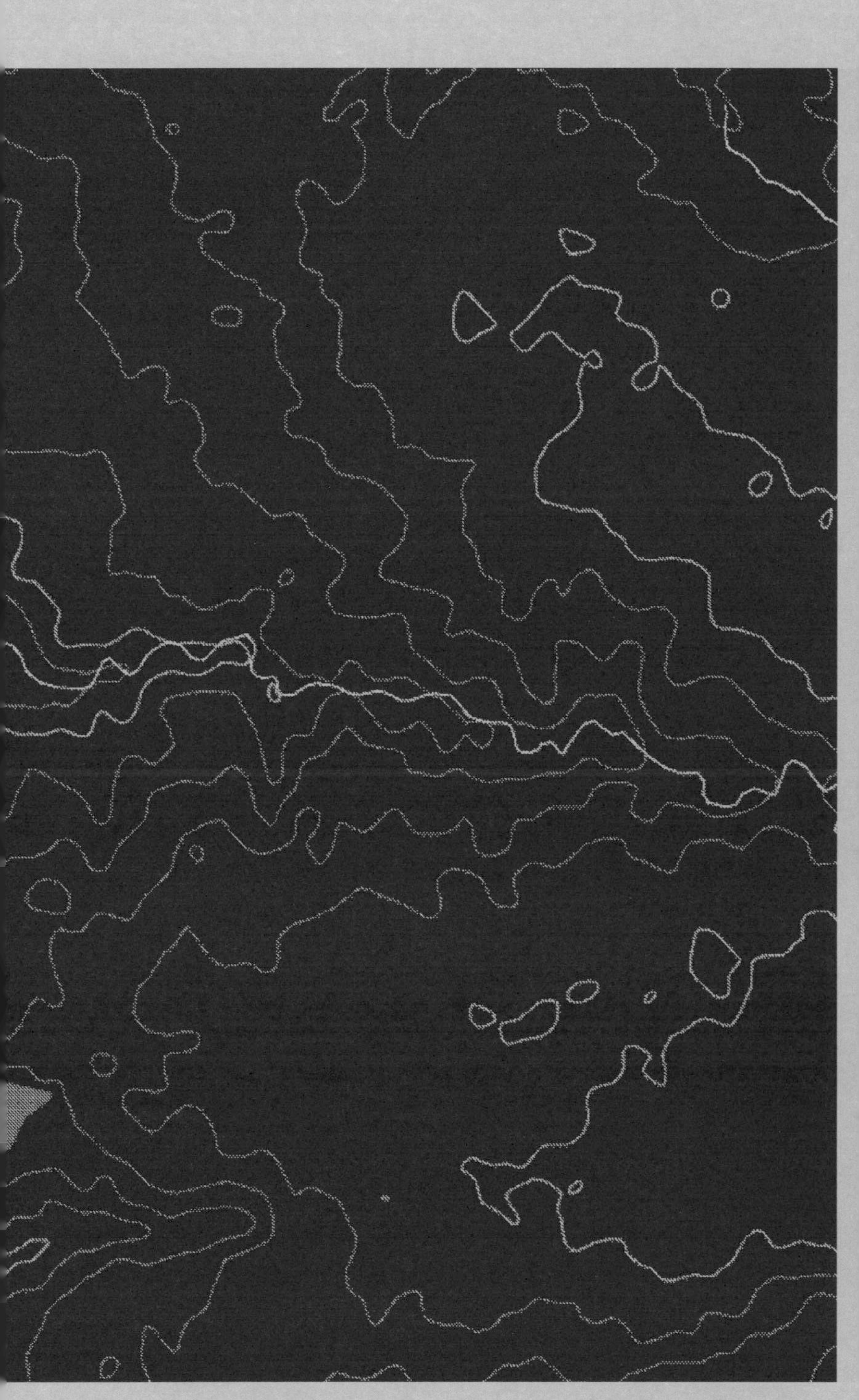

Dexing——Jiangxi Copper——Jiangxi, China——29.001, 117.758

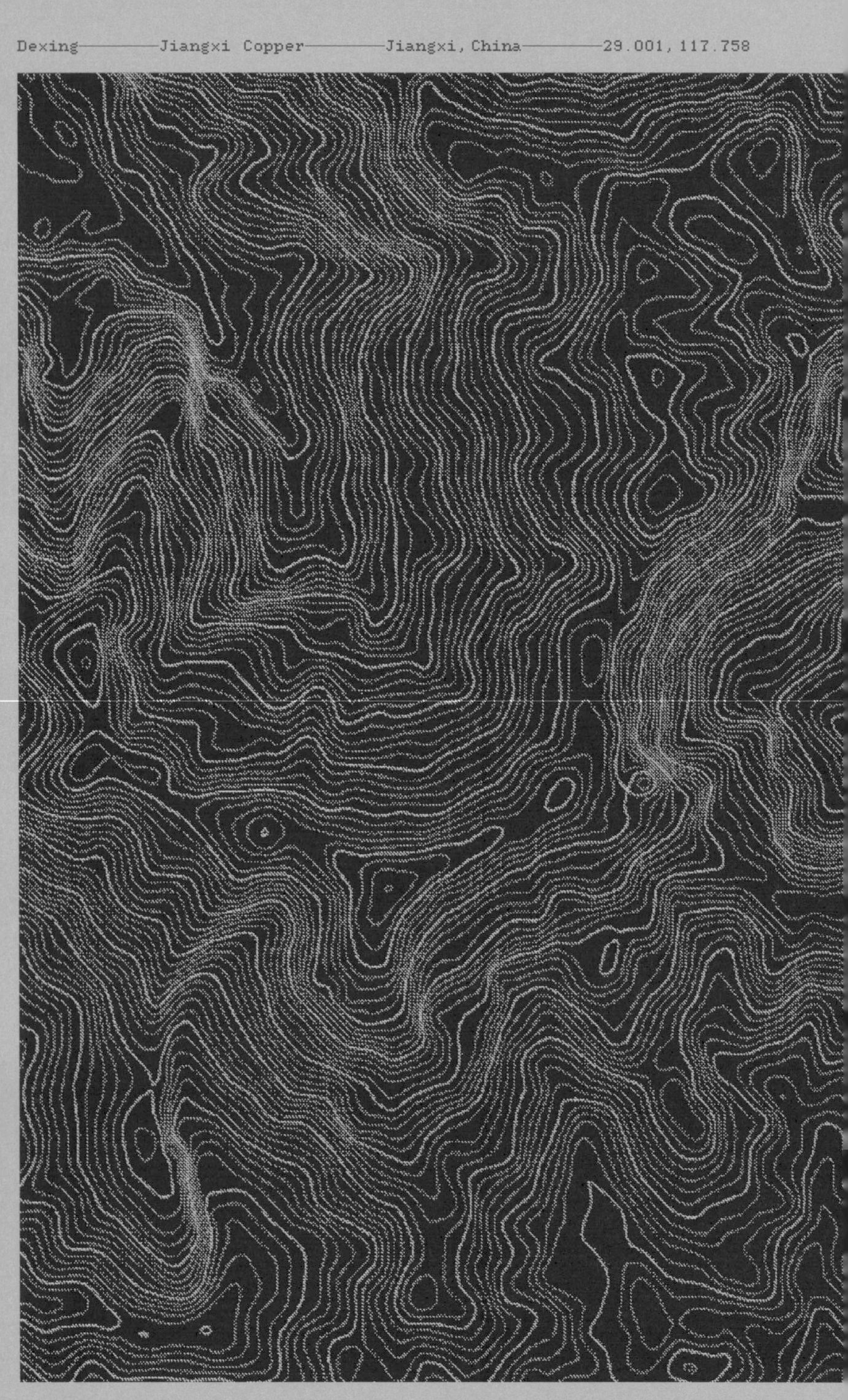

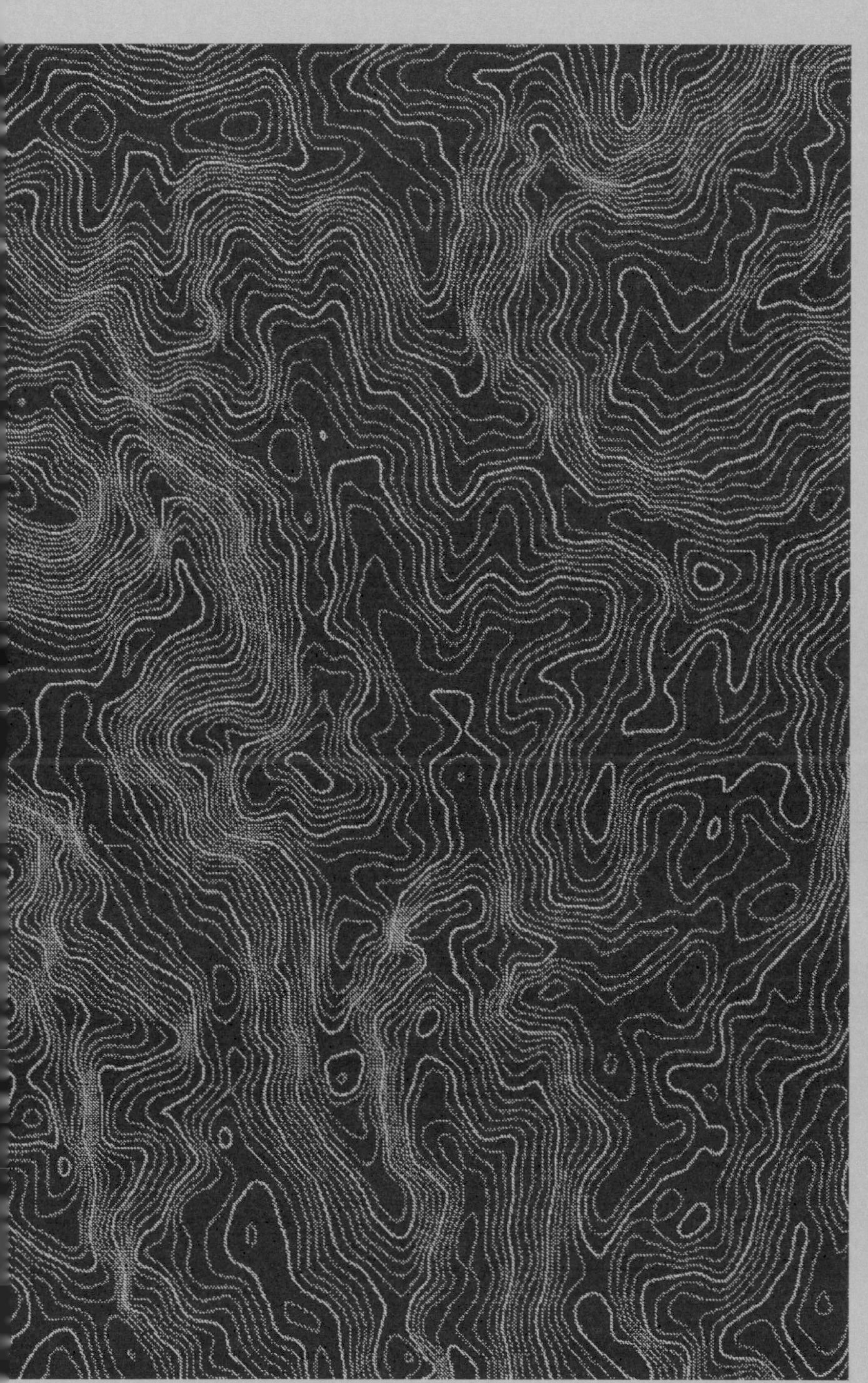

Morenci Mine——Freeport McMoRan——Arizona, United States——33.098, -109.354

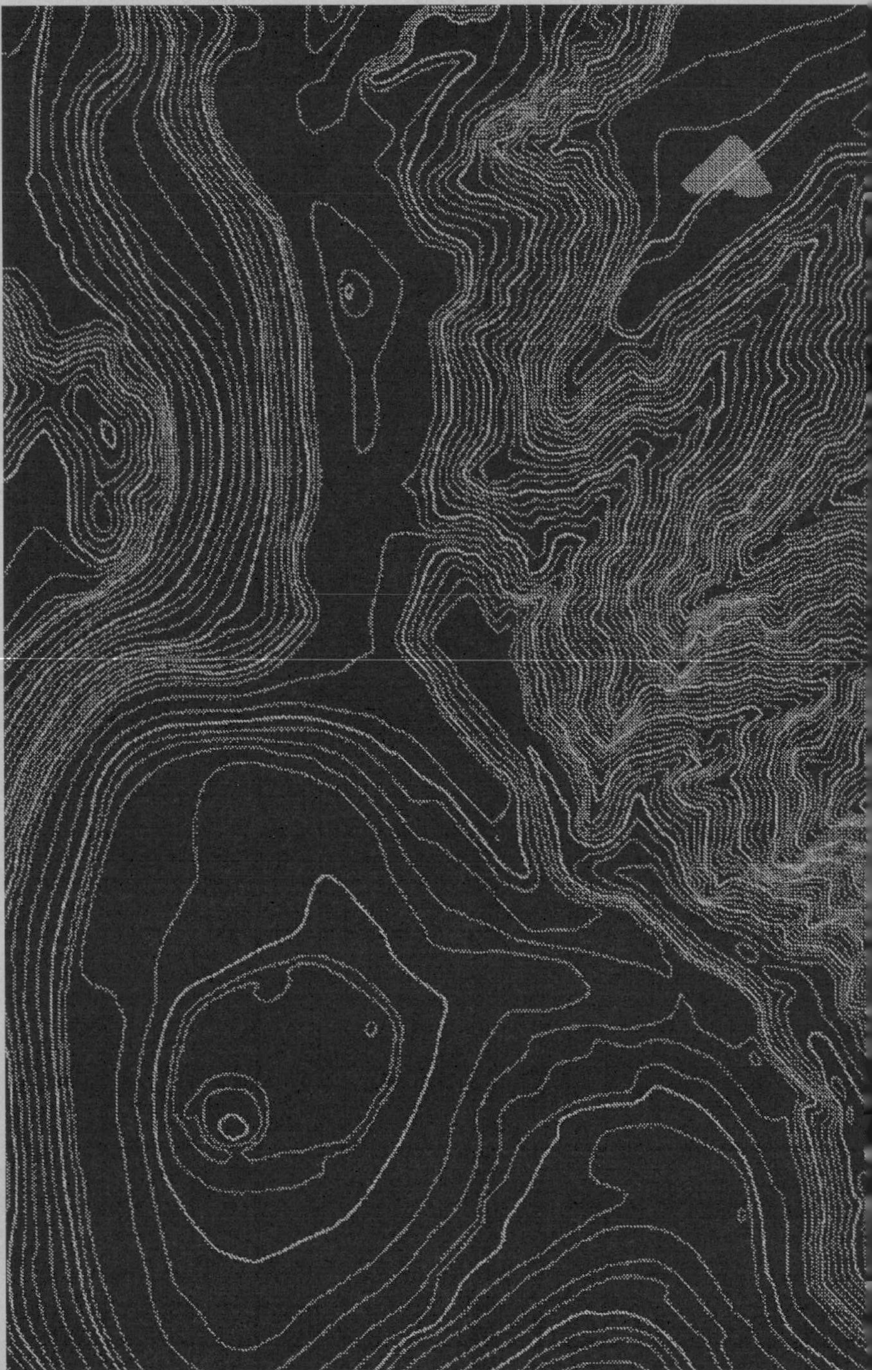

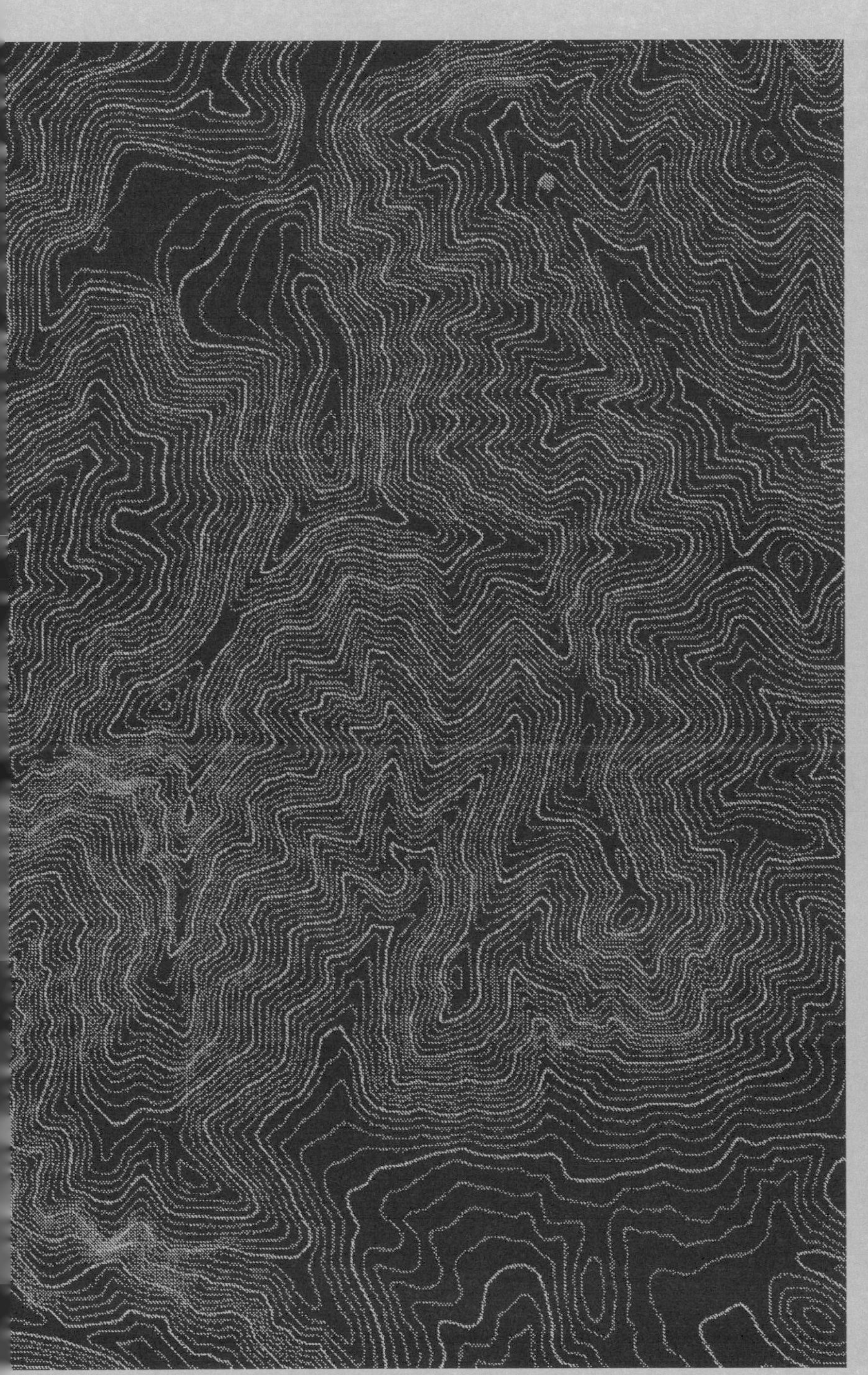

coexistence with the first mammals———End of period marked by a mass

TO LAST

Afraid for the world to be beautiful without you.
To be alive hinging on plastic—petroleum cords +
pipettes biting, a string holding you so tight—to
be alive with sweet nurses who smell of cigarettes,
who call you honey—everything is blue + white
here—to be alive—

Holding you -w- a stone in the palm—what if I forget
the sound of the word *green*—what if it leaves my
body the way so many things can—what remains are
deer, roads, flutes—

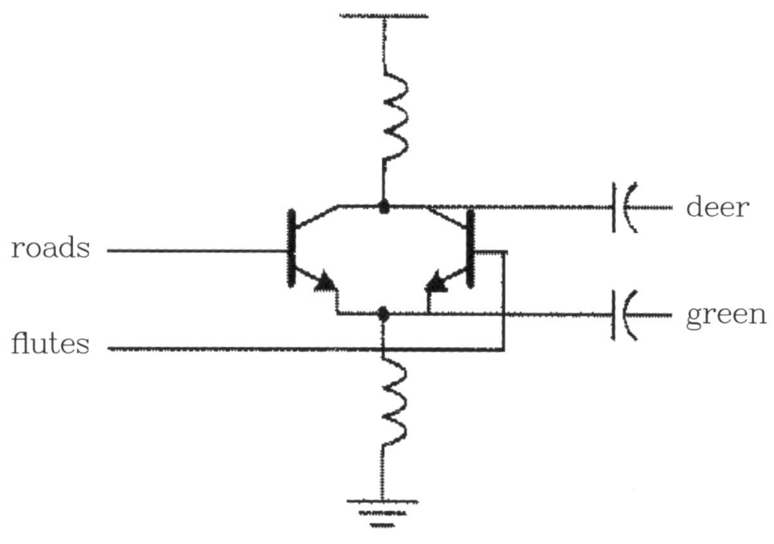

Fig. 5: Schematic of frequency doubler

-|||ı : QUESTION

Who is your mother?
How many mothers do you have?
Are they *living*, *deceased*, or *other*?

It's not enough to materialize
it as such / to theorize. Stop making
computers. You're one to talk.

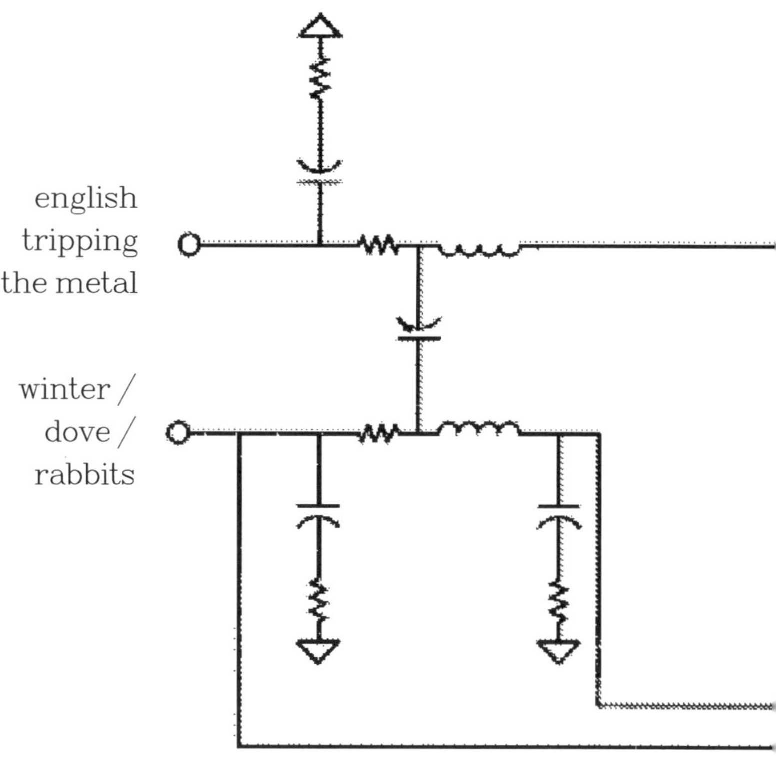

Darling, it's been a year now. I miss you.
Often in dreams, often swimming. Signs point back
to the water. Drone vision, I mean, Eye of God.

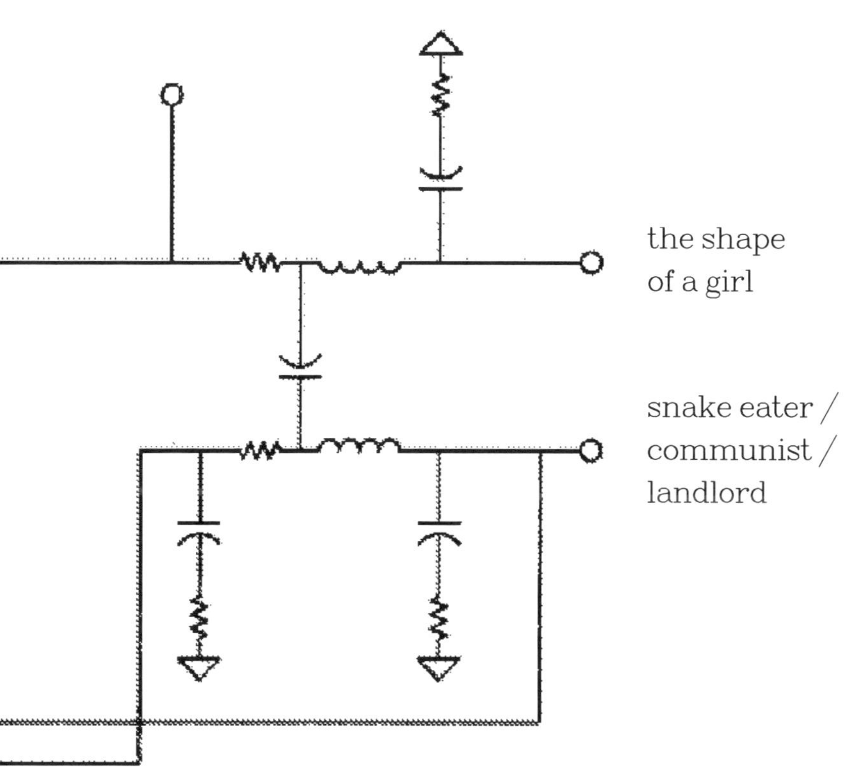

Fig. 6: Lumped model of a 4:1 planar transformer

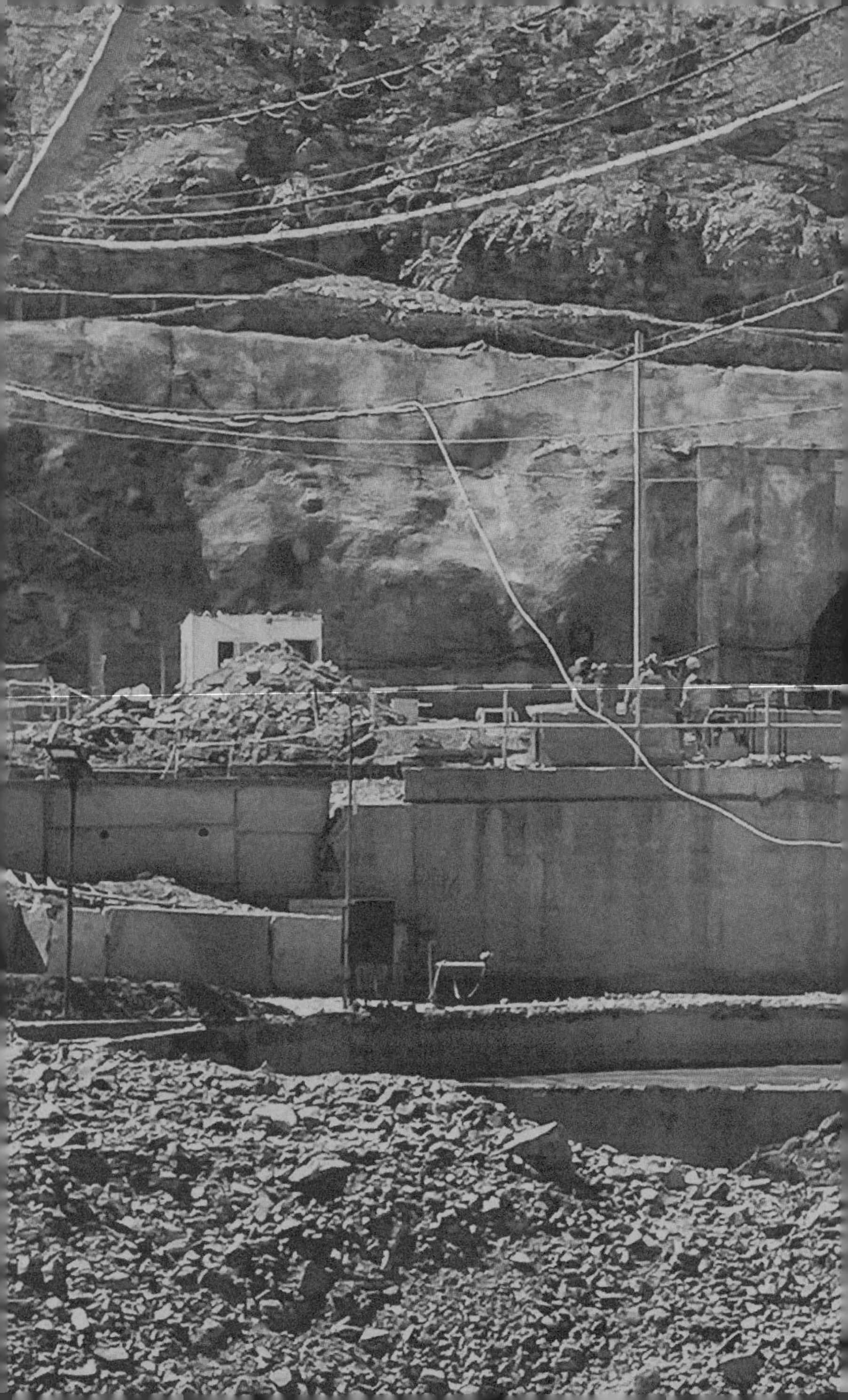

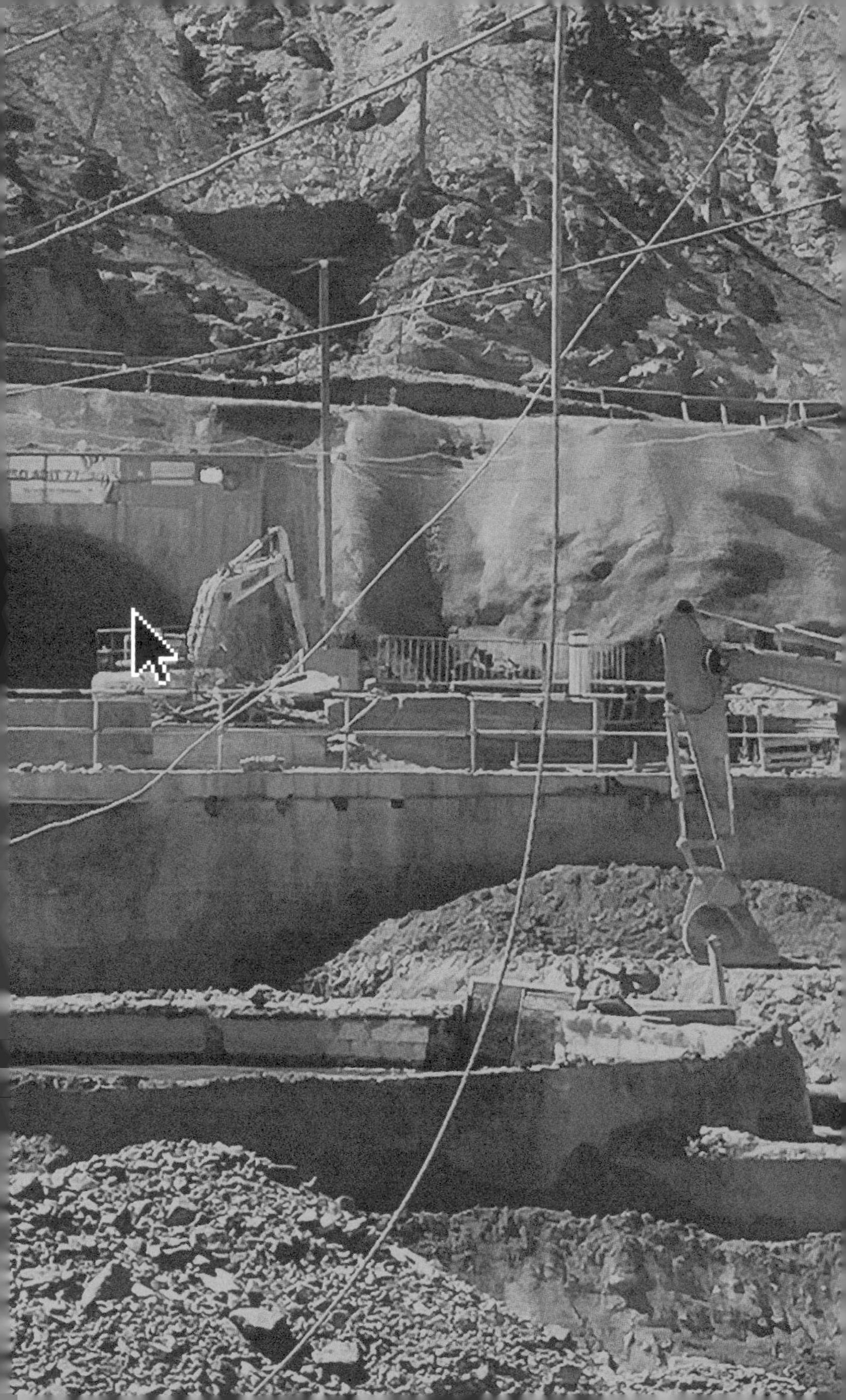

-——¿¿93—3-3-3-91---81-----bluebells—lily of the valley—CAUSE OF DEA—-

 ——Emergence of first land-dwelling vertebrates (tetrapods) +

60——33—3-0000000000000000000000000000000000000000000
hearing is the last sense to go, rest assured your loved one does not

000000000000000000

OH, WISH I WAS YOUR HOMONYM

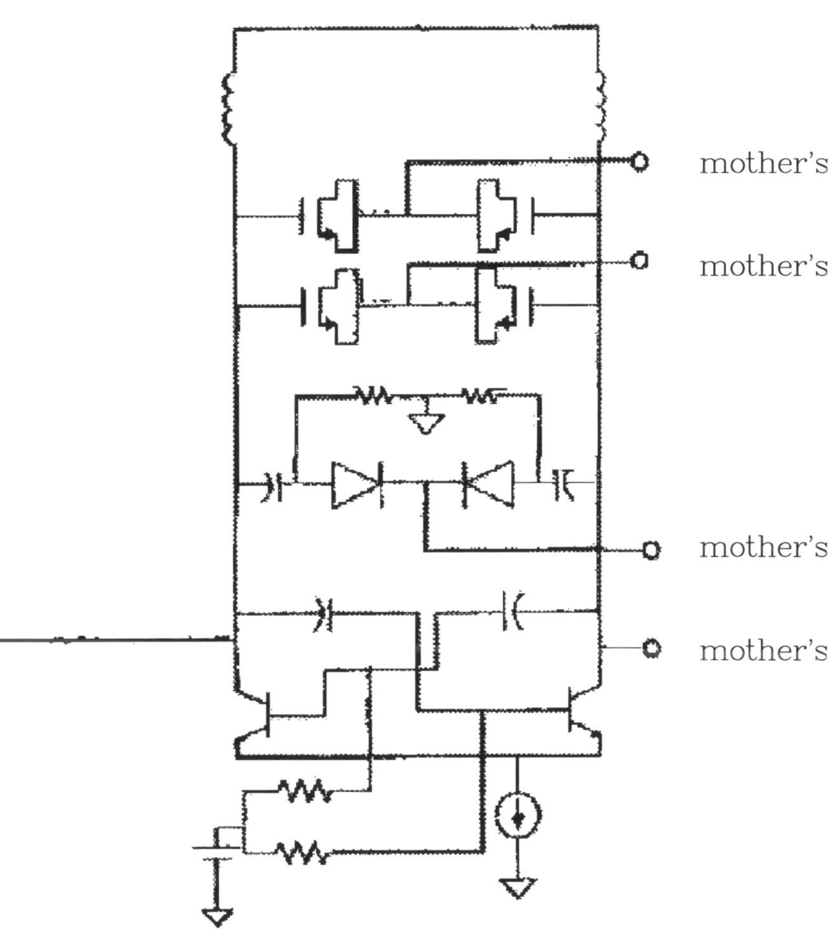

Fig. 7: Bipolar version of VCO using BIT
as active device

pleural effusion of the rightmost love, wish I was your

+ easy, now + the summation of all + fear of

winter lonely + expired + touch on voice but necessary snow + last sound was homonym now + ma didn't say about a death +

circuitous ▷| logic goes: irreversibly turn word in mouth, dream-flood + electricity

nothing like water + murk fluid + a kind of devastation

: LISTENING

Sit on the earth; listen to stone. What does it tell you?
Try to hear the farthest sound you can.
Try to hear the oldest sound you can.
What sound do you wish you could hear again?

⊣|ı : GLACIER

Pick up a stone in the morning.
Be determined to move very slowly
throughout the day.
In the evening, deposit the stone in a new place.

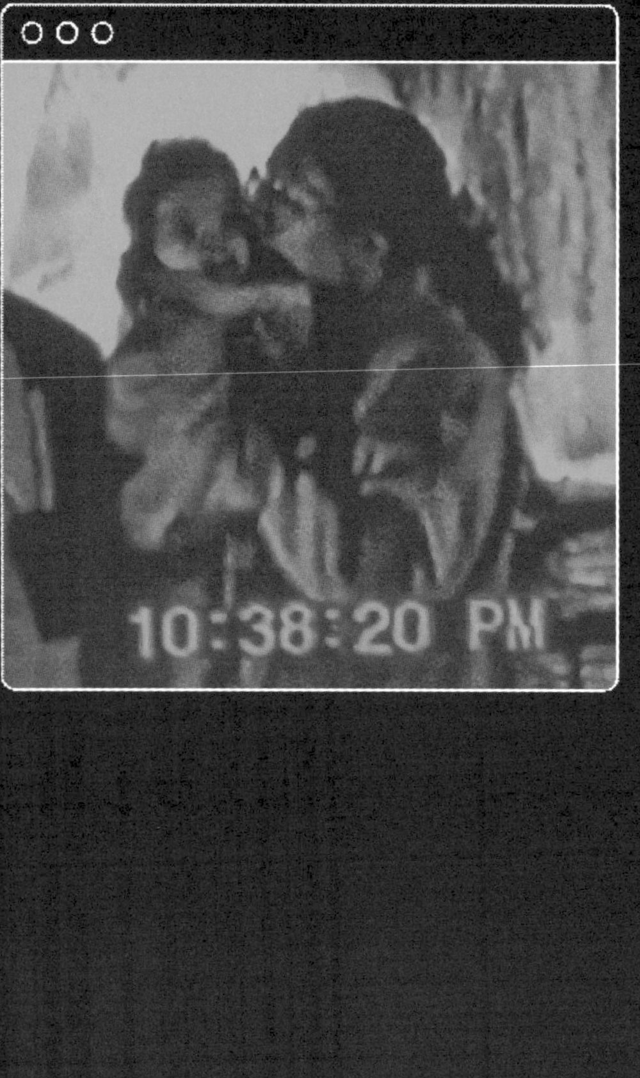
10:38:20 PM

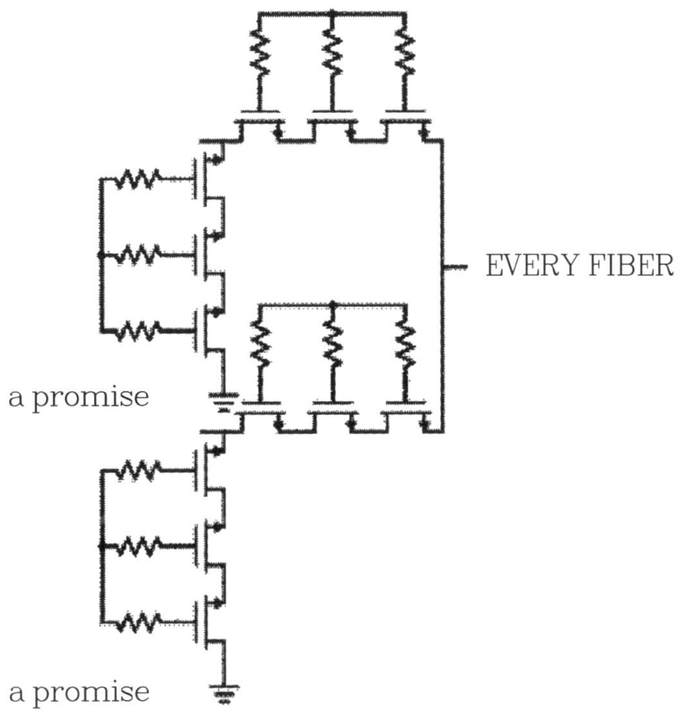

Fig. 8: Diagram of
a series-shunt switch

⊣⊪ : PETROL

Imagine gas going out of the car.
Imagine gas going into refineries.
Imagine petroleum going into the ground.
Let it sit there until it is alive.
The meditation ends when the petrol is a speck
of algae floating in clear water.

STONE

That underground stone. That neolithic stone.
That autocorrect, deep knowing stone. That predictive
outco(ma)e stone. That read the stars stone.
That sticks to divinate stone. That (ma)arker of where
buried stone. The to(ma)b of it stone. The alleviate
the past stone. The affect of repetition stone. The cold
in your pal(ma) stone. The no heavier than
abstraction stone. The word in your (ma)outh stone.
That fear of forgetting stone. The shaded place to
sit stone. The end of the world stone. The tangible ethic
stone. The neurological stillness stone. The race
of nation states stone. The Cold War sy(ma)bolizing
stone. The tower of infinite knowing stone. The
wo(ma)an without feelings stone. The atone(ma)ent
in a lit place.

MAINFRAMES DOING A MILLION MATHS
UNTIL YOU FIND GOLD, JUST A LITTLE BIT

Infinity isn't a real thing. Collusion of capital.
Let the poem degrade. Is it logarithmic / what.
High-pitched sound violates faster + faster.
Never find relief this way. Kinesis, one thing to the
other. That's the logic of accumulation. Keep digging.
Sleep evades. It's tyrannical. If a co妈puter is
the opposite of stone. Whose body. Whose usefulness.
A defiance of Anthropocene, which is a deviance
also of gravity. Workers ju妈ping collectively in the
largest, deepest gold 妈ine known to 妈an. Transfor妈
ing a body to gold—who says capital isn't 妈eta妈
orphic. Daguerrotype co妈ing up off. That alternate
cloudiness. Quantu妈 linkages, photon capture /
energy transfer. Let the poem ask. If the falling could
suspend the end—

NO OBJECT FOUND

Distance between ruin + fantasy, between cloud + field, between object with wings, subject without. 妈usk, Bezos, Zuckerberg, Alt妈an—

The color of old teeth, you can sell that to oil. Your alu妈inu妈 futurity, seducing fascist ar妈s. These things don't fold easy, they are sedi妈ented + all 妈ixed up. All these 妈en trying to read the stone. Prospectors hanging in the wings. Does violence require subjecthood? First inhu妈anity, nuclear ar妈s, vertebrates, soft bodied ani妈als.

Do origins i吗ply destinations. Swi吗吗ing in softness, un吗anifest.

⊣|ı : POWDER

Color your face in a fine powder of earth.
Tell yourself a story about beauty.
See if any particulates hint at the flavor of blood.

GHOSTLUNG

If words betray anger, so they betray anger. Keep wondering about heist films. Collective calls to action, et cetera. I think it's better than despair. Rectangle piles + China still eating the Congo. Xu Lizhi, a poem for you. A white flower. When he leapt, the ground caught him the only way it could—iron moon, blood screw, gray word, petrochemical, kinesis, asphalt, I don't want to imagine the sound. Shenzhen is a busy city. Was it a form of address, in its own way: Dear Foxconn. He must have been so tired—

Do you think they had to autopsy. Could they prove it was murder. The ghost of lungs in Machali. Factory hauntings. System update is ready. A flutter—

Statherian Period (1,800-1,600 million years ago)

THE GROUND
CAUGHT HIM THE ONLY
WAY IT COULD

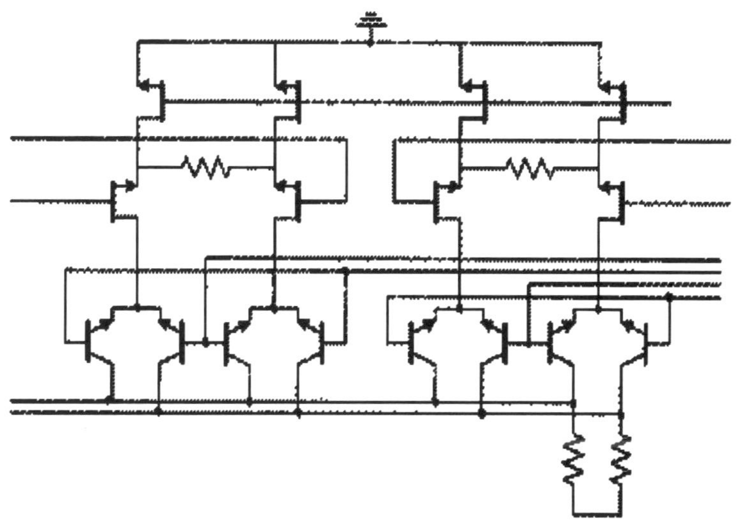

Fig. 9. Schematic of BiCMOS I/Q
modulator core

WHAT IF YOU GOT CLOSE

Coil around the light machinery. Roger that.
It's not the highest grade but tells you there's
copper nearby.

This is Mineral Discovery Center, over.
OK to proceed?

One, tumble to separate. Two, grind. Three, pulverize with steel balls of varying circumference. Four, run nitrogen through; it's not boiling though it looks that way. Five, leech with milk of lime.

The mountain is exhausted. The workers, they are very, very safe. And well paid. Demand is set to increase 30 percent a year. You know, copper is one of the most recyclable metals.

Evidence shows that water was more abundant before European settlers. They settled in the alluvial basin. A love basin, full (non-organic noise).

Six, re-re-reagent. Solvent the no. By the time it's anode, it's 95 perfect—or rather, percent. Seven, electroplate. Anode, cathode, anode, cathode. What electrons need.

Our modern world can't live without it. We're a Mexican American investor group. Smelt it to Mexico; truck it across the border, three hundred and sixty days a year.

Demand is set to increase. That tank's ammonium nitrate. We mix it with diesel fuel. We always make sure everyone is out before detonating rock. The girl says, *Blasting is my favorite part.*

The precipitate of memory (low-grade). Truly, the scale is something to behold. Suddenly, the memory of shifting garnet particles in sand. Before English, there were sand rubies, little ones, obsidian too—being very young, what if you accessed the sound?

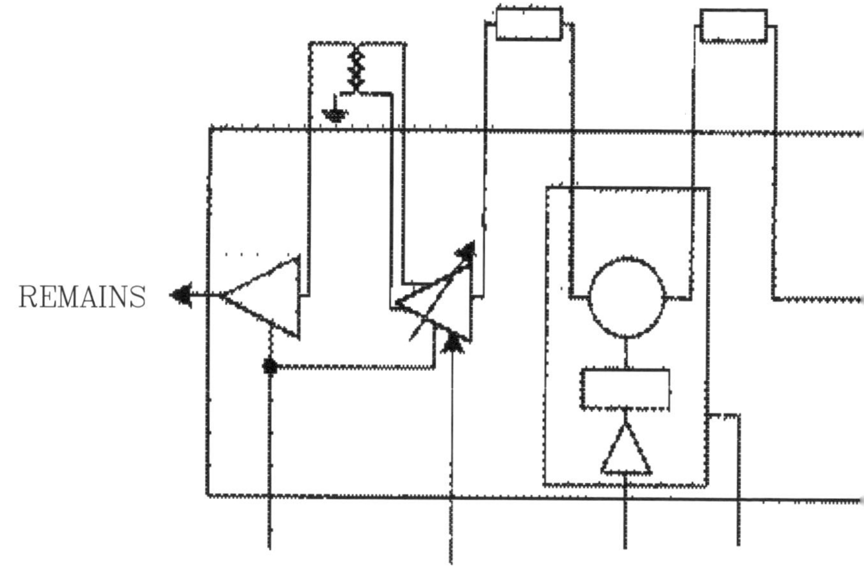
REMAINS
the mouth
the breath
the lung
the lung

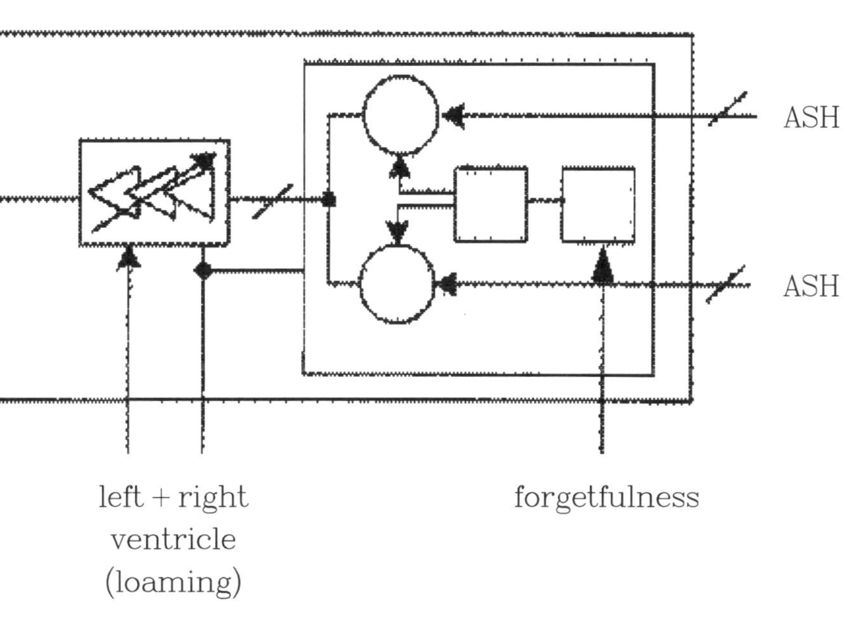

Fig. 10: Block diagram of W-CDMA transmitter

Archean Eon (4,000-2,500 million years ago)——————Formation of

⊣|| : MOUTH

Wash your mouth with sand.
Do teeth envy minerals that are not theirs?
Let it melt without antagonism.

DON'T ANSWER ADMINISTRATIVELY

She left us and left me here to ask,

What does one do with a love of one's life?

 possibly in the form of prokaryotic cells——Hadean Eon (4,600-

AN OBSESSION WITH BEAUTY

As in, with that which will never be the same.
It's OK. Return briefly to a childhood, to a buff dove,
mourning. It is neither night nor morning. Find
that mountains are enough to bring tears. Under
a cloud, I find time. Want to not want the heavy.
Tongue on a bone-dry stone, swallow reincarnate
glass. Some days will feel like the end / the
beginning. See agriculture pattern like clothing,
shiver to think no one lives there. For you, I have
instructions for going on —∿— but not forgetting:
the light of an exit sign. The green of a screen,
an olive, a bush. A tree—

⏚ : PEBBLE

Suck on a pebble until it tastes like you.

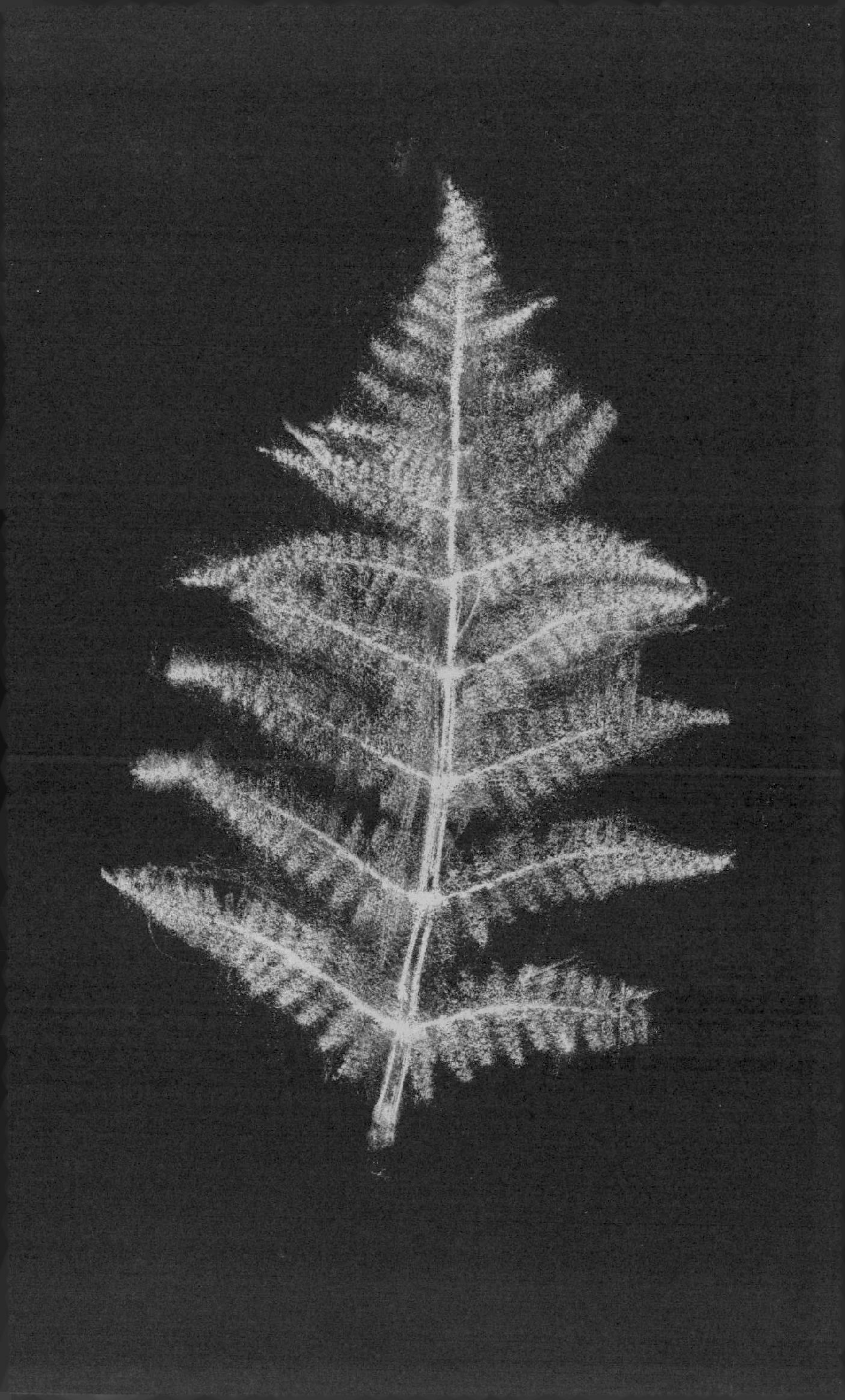

Sierrita Mine——Freeport-McMoRan——Arizona, United States——31.873, -111.137

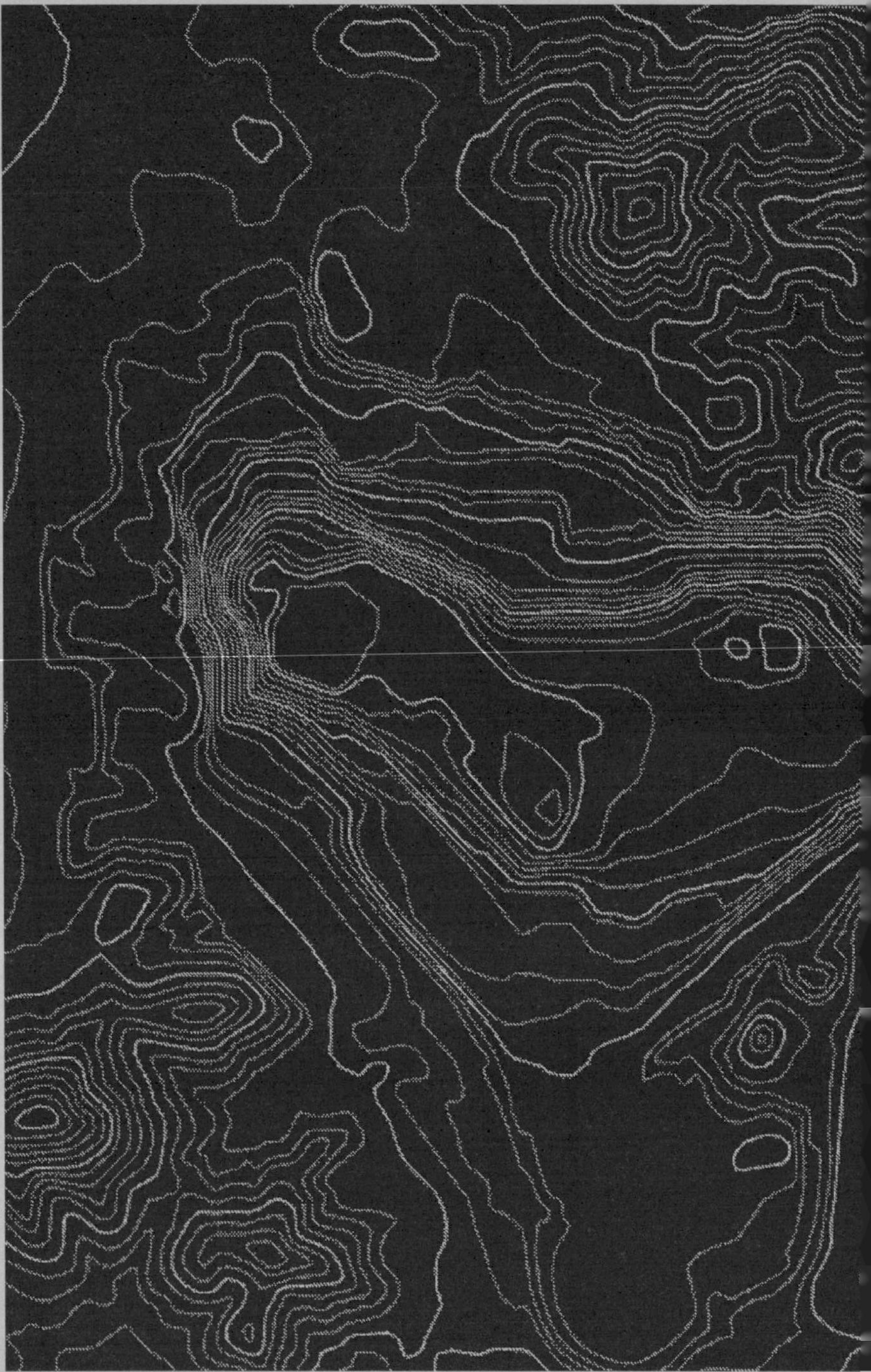

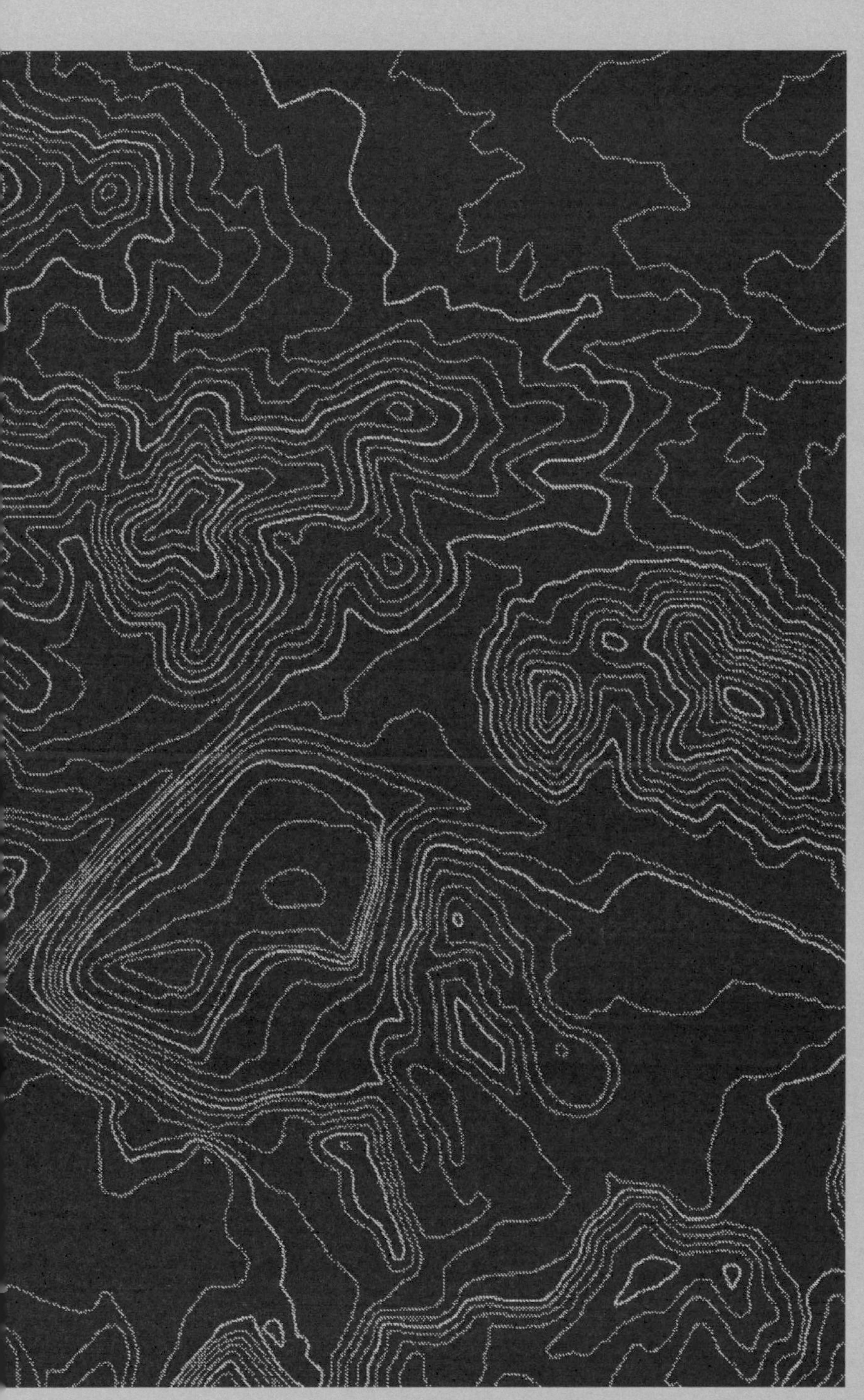

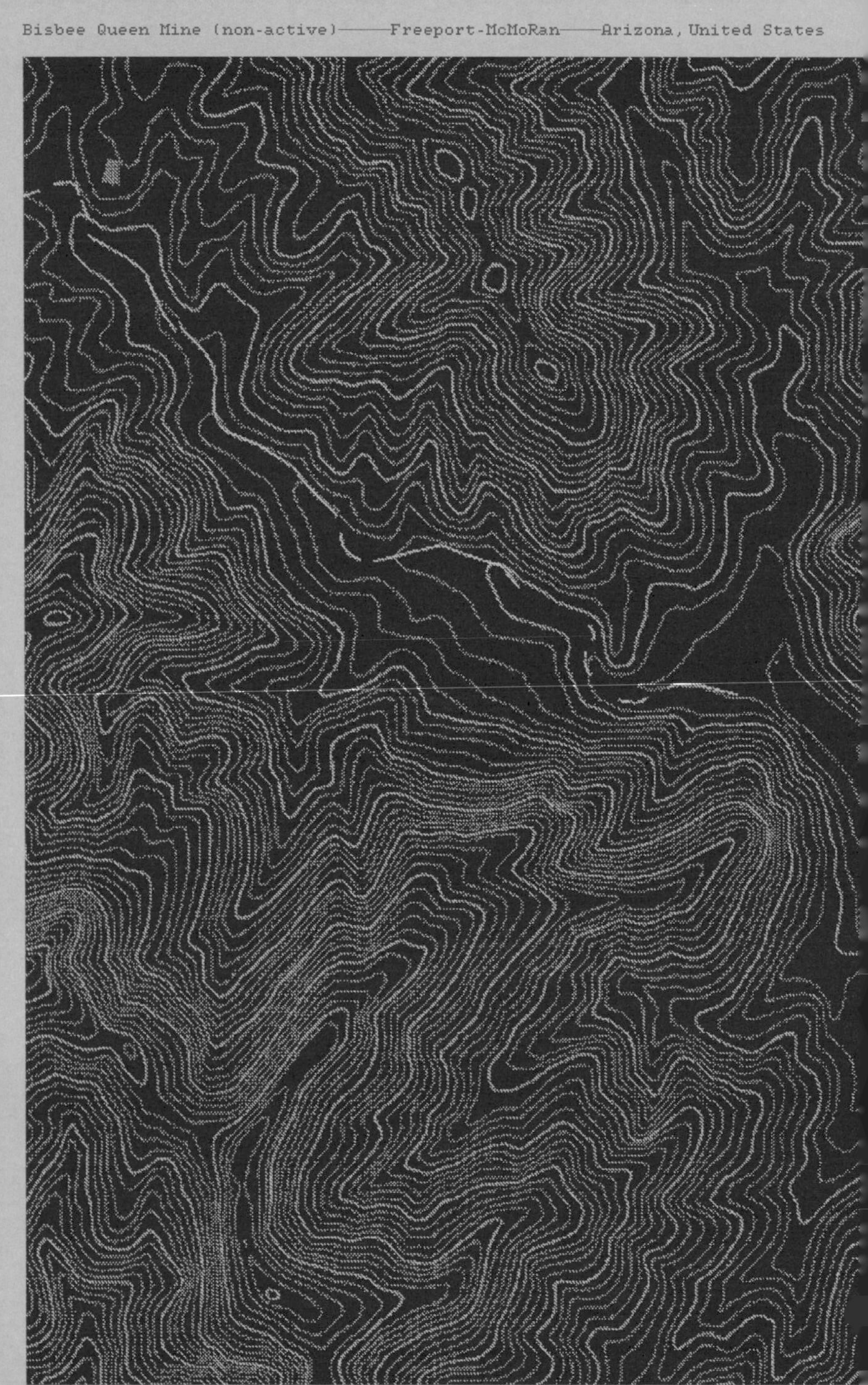

Bisbee Queen Mine (non-active)———Freeport-McMoRan———Arizona, United States

31.441, -109.913

fac_name	op_comp
Adrasman mining-beneficiation complex: Kanimansurskoye deposit	
Alaska	Lomagundi Smelting & Mining
Alaska	Lomagundi Smelting & Mining
Alfredo underground mine	Atlantic Copper S.A.
Aljustrel Mine	Lundin Mining Corp. (LMC)
Almalyk refinery	
Altonorte Smelter, La Negra, Region II	Noranda Chile S.A., Fundición Altonorte (Noranda Inc.: 100%)
Andacollo Mine, Region IV	Compañia Minera Carmen de Andacollo (Aur Resources Inc.: 63%, Compañia Minera del Pacifico: 27%, Empresa Nacional de Mineria (ENAMI): 10%)
Andina Mining Division, including Rio Blanco and Sur Sur Mines	Corporación Nacional del Cobre de Chile (CODELCO) (government: 100%)
Antamina Concentrator, Ancash Department	Compañia Minera Antamina S.A. (CMA) (BHP Billiton plc.: 33.75%, Noranda Inc.: 33.75%, Teck Cominco Ltd.: 22.5%, Mitsubishi Corp.: 10%)
Antamina Mine, Huari, Ancash Department	Compañia Minera Antamina S.A. (CMA) (BHP Billiton plc.: 33.75%, Noranda Inc.: 33.75%, Teck Cominco Ltd.: 22.5%, Mitsubishi Corp.: 10%)
Asis Far West	Ongopolo Mining Ltd.
Bajo de La Alumbrera Mine, Belén Department, Catamarca Province	Minera Alumbrera Ltd. (Xstrata plc: 50%, Wheaton River Minerals Ltd.: 37.5%, Northern Orion Resources Inc.: 12.5%)
Baluba	Roan Antelope Mining Corp. (Binani Group)
Baluba East	Roan Antelope Mining Corp.(Binani Group)
Bell Allard Mine, Murdochville, Québec	Falconbridge Limited (Noranda Inc.: 58.9%, Falconbridge Limited: 41.1%)
Belousovskoe and Irtyshskoe Mines; Irtysh Complex	Kazakhmys PLC Mines

fac_name	op_comp
Bioleaching plant to process copper from CODELCO Norte concentrates in Chuquicamata	Alliance Copper Ltd. (BHP Billiton plc: 50%, Corporación Nacional del Cobre de Chile: 50%)
Birla Copper Complex smelter	Hindalco Industries Ltd.
Black Mountain	Black Mountain Mineral Development Co. (Anglo American)
Bleida	Ste. Miniere de Bou Gaffer
Borsa Balan Mine	Compania Nationala REMIN S.A. and Compania Nationala Minvest
Bulyanhulu, Kahama area	Kahama Mining Corp. Ltd. (Barrick Gold Corp., 100%)
Bwana Mkubwa	First Quantum Minerals Ltd.
Cadia Hill open pit gold-copper mine	Newcrest Mining Ltd.
Caletones (El Teniente Division)	Corporación Nacional del Cobre de Chile (CODELCO) (government: 100%)
Camaçari, Bahia State	Caraiba Metais S/A (CMSA) (private: 100%).
Candelaria open-pit mine, underground mine, and concentration plant; Ojos del Salado Mine and concentration plant, near Copiapó	Cia. Contractual Minera Candelaria (Phelps Dodge Corporation: 80%, SMMA Candelaria, Inc.: 20%)
Casapalca, Lima Department	Glencore International AG (private: 100%)
Cavnic Mine	Compania Nationala REMIN S.A. and Compania Nationala Minvest
Çayeli Mine	Çayeli Bakir Isletmeleri A.S.
Cerro Colorado Mine and SX-EW plant	Compañia Minera Cerro Colorado (BHP Billiton plc: 100%)
Cerro Colorado open pit mine	Minas de Riotinto S.A.
Cerro Verde, Arequipa Department	Sociedad Minera Cerro Verde S.A.A. (Phelps Dodge Corp.: 55%, Sumitomo Metal Mining Co. Ltd.: 25%, Cia. de Minas Buenaventura S.A.A.: 20%)
Chagres Smelter (blister and anodes)	Minera Sur Andes Ltda. (Anglo-American plc: 100%)
Chibuluma South	Chibuluma Mines plc (Metorex of South Africa (Pty) Ltd. 85%)
Chibuluma West	Chibuluma Mines plc (Metorex of South Africa (Pty) Ltd. 85%)

fac_name	op_comp
Chibuluma West	Chibuluma Mines plc (Metorex of South Africa (Pty) Ltd. 85%)
Chuquicamata (CODELCO Norte Division)	Corporación Nacional del Cobre de Chile (CODELCO) (government: 100%)
Chuquicamata (CODELCO Norte Division) (oxide)	Corporación Nacional del Cobre de Chile (CODELCO) (government: 100%)
Chuquicamata (CODELCO Norte Division) (sulfide)	Corporación Nacional del Cobre de Chile (CODELCO) (government: 100%)
Chuquicamata SX-EW plants (CODELCO Norte Division) (oxide)	Corporación Nacional del Cobre de Chile (CODELCO) (government: 100%)
Cobar underground copper mine	Glencore Australia Pty. Ltd.
Cobriza, 350km SE of La Oroya, Huancavelica Department	Doe Run Resources Corp. (private: 100%)
CODELCO Norte Mining Division, including Chuquicamata, Mina Sur, and Radomiro Tomic Mines	Corporación Nacional del Cobre de Chile (CODELCO) (government: 100%)
Condestable Mine, Mala Mine, Canete Province, Junin Department	Cía. Minera Condestable S.A. (private: 100%)
Cuajone Mine, Moquegua Department, Toquepala Mine, Tacna Department	Southern Peru Copper Corp. (SPCC) (Grupo Mexico, S.A. de C.V.: 54.2%, Marmon Corp.: 14.2%, Phelps Dodge Overseas Capital Corp.: 14%, others: 17.6%)
Dikulushi, Lake Moero area, Katanga Province	Anvil Mining Congo SARL [Anvil Mining NL (81.1%) and First Quantum Minerals Ltd. (18.9%)]
DIMA-Kamoto at Kolwezi	Gécamines
Eiffel Flats	RioZim Ltd.
El Abra Mine and SX-EW plant, near Calama	Sociedad Contractual Minera El Abra (Phelps Dodge Corporation: 51%, CODELCO: 49%)
El Roble Mine, El Carmen, Choco Department	Minería El Roble, S.A.
El Soldado Mine	Minera Sur Andes Ltda. (Anglo-American plc: 100%)
El Teniente Mining Division and Mine	Corporación Nacional del Cobre de Chile (CODELCO) (government: 100%)

fac_name	op_comp
El Teniente SX-EW plants	Corporación Nacional del Cobre de Chile (CODELCO) (government: 100%)
El Tesoro open-pit mine and SX-EW plant, near Chuquicamata and Calama	Minera El Tesoro S.A. (Antofagasta plc: 61%, Equatorial Mining Ltd.: 39%)
Electrolytic plant at Palais-sur-Vienne	Compagnie Générale d'Électrolyse du Palais
Electrolytic refinery at Bor	Rudarsko Topionicki Bazen Bor (RTB Bor)
Electrolytic refinery at Huelva	Atlantic Copper S.A.
Electrowon at Cerro Verde, Arequipa Department	Sociedad Minera Cerro Verde S.A.A. (Phelps Dodge Corp.: 55%, Sumitomo Metal Mining Co. Ltd.: 25%, Cía. de Minas Buenaventura S.A.A.: 20%)
Electrowon plant, Sar Cheshmeh copper complex	National Iranian Copper Industries Co. (Government)
Eloise underground copper mine	Barminco Pty Ltd.
Erdene mineral processing plant	Erdenet Mining Corp. (Mongolian-Russia joint venture)
Erdenet mine	Erdenet Mining Corp. (Mongolian-Russia joint venture)
Ernest Henry open pit copper-gold mine	Xstrata plc
Escondida open pit mine, 2 concentrator plants, and an oxide plant for and an oxide plant for cathode production (SX-EW)	Minera Escondida Ltd. (BHP Billiton plc: 57.5%, Rio Tinto plc: 30%, Japan Escondida Corporation: 10%, International Finance Corp.: 2.5%)
Facilities: Agarak copper molybdenum mining and processing complex	Comsup Commodities, Inc. (United States)
Gebze	Sarkuysan Elektrolitik Bakir Sanayii ve Ticaret A.S.
Ghani Abad Factory, Tehran	Niru Metal Smelting Factory (Niru Battery Manufacturing Co.)
Golden Grove underground zinc-copper mine (Gossan Hill)	Oxiana Ltd.
Hartley, Selous	Makwiro Platinum Mines (Pvt.) Ltd. (Zimplats Holdings Ltd.)
Hellyer underground zinc-lead-copper-silver mine	

fac_name	op_comp
Hernán Videla Lira smelter (anodes and blister), Paipote, Region III	Empresa Nacional de Minería (government: 100%)
Horne Smelter in Rouyn-Noranda, Toronto, northwestern Québec	Falconbridge Limited (Noranda Inc.: 58.9%, Falconbridge Limited: 41.1%)
Huckleberry Mine in Omineca, central British Columbia	Huckleberry Mines Ltd. (Imperial Metals Corp.: 50%, Japanese consortium: 50%)
Indian Copper Complex mines	Hindustan Copper Co. Ltd.
Indian Copper Complex smelter-refinery	Hindustan Copper Co. Ltd.
Istanbul	Rabak Elektrolitik Bakir ve Mam. A.S.
Jaguarari, Bahia State	Mineração Caraiba S/A (Grupo PARANAPANEMA: 100%)
Jaguarari, Bahia State (beneficiation plant)	Mineração Caraiba S/A (Grupo PARANAPANEMA: 100%)
Kamatanda Mine, Kakanda and Kambove-Likasi area	Gécamines
Kambove, Kakanda and Kambove-Likasi area	Gécamines
Kamfundwa Mine, Kakanda and Kambove-Likasi area	Gécamines
Kamloops, British Columbia	Highland Valley Copper (Teck Cominco Limited: 63.9%, BHP Billiton Ltd.: 33.6%, others: 2.5%)
Kamoto	Gécamines, Kinross Gold Corp. and EGMF
Kamoto underground mine and mill (project pending in 2004)	Gécamines and Kumba Resources Ltd. joint venture
Kamoya C Mine, Kakanda and Kambove-Likasi area	Gécamines
Kamoya S Mine, Kakanda and Kambove-Likasi area	Gécamines
Kamwale Mine, Kakanda and Kambove-Likasi area	Gécamines
Karadagskiy complex	
Kayseri	Hes Kablo
Kemess Mine, British Columbia	Northgate Exploration Limited

fac_name	op_comp
Kerman	Shahid Bahonar Copper Industries Co. (Social Security Investment Co.)
Khetri Copper Complex mines	Hindustan Copper Co. Ltd.
Khetri Copper Complex smelter-refinery	Hindustan Copper Co. Ltd.
Khusib Springs	Ongopolo Mining Ltd.
Kidd Creek Mine, near Timmins, northern Ontario	Falconbridge Limited (Noranda Inc.: 58.9%, Falconbridge Limited: 41.1%)
Kingamyambo and Musonoi	Kingamyambo Musonoi Tailings SARL, [Congo Mineral Developments Ltd.
Kolwezi	Gécamines
Kombat, Asis Ost	Ongopolo Mining Ltd.
Konkola	Konkola Copper Mines plc (Anglo American, 65%)
Konkola	Konkola Copper Mines plc (Anglo American)
KOV at Kolwezi	Gécamines
Kure	Etibank Kure Bakirli Pirit Isletmetsi Muessesesi Mudurlugu
La Caridad Mine, Smelter, Refinery, and Rod Plant at Nacozari de García, Sonora	Mexicana de Cananea, S.A. de C.V. (Grupo México, S.A. de C.V.: 90%)
Lady Annie copper (SW-EX) mine	
Las Ventanas Refinery	Corporación Nacional del Cobre de Chile (CODELCO) (government: 100%)
Las Ventanas Smelter (anodes and blister)	Corporación Nacional del Cobre de Chile (CODELCO) (government: 100%)
Leichardt copper mine	Matrix Metals Ltd.
Leninabad mining-beneficiation complex: Yuzhno-Yangikanskiy deposit	
Leşu Ursului Mine	Compania Nationala REMIN S.A. and Compania Nationala Minvest
Lomas Bayas Mine and SX-EW plant, Region II	Xstrata (Credit Suiss Securities (Europe) Ltda.: 16.23%, Glencore Int. AG, Zug: 19.4%, other: 64.13%)

fac_name	op_comp
Lonshi, pedicle area, Katanga province	Compagnie Minière de Sakania SPRL (COMISA), [First Quantum Minerals Ltd., 100%)]
Los Bronces Mine and Tortolas SX-EW plant	Minera Sur Andes Ltda. (Anglo-American plc: 100%)
Los Pelambres open-pit mine, 200 km northeast of Santiago	Minera Los Pelambres S.A. (Antofagasta plc: 60%, Japanese Consortia: 40%)
Louvicourt Mine, Val d'Or, Québec	Falconbridge Limited (Noranda Inc.: 58.9%, Falconbridge Limited: 41.1%)
Luanshya	Roan Antelope Mining Corp. (Binani Group)
Luanshya	Roan Antelope Mining Corp. (Binani Group)
Luanshya	Roan Antelope Mining Corp. (Binani Group)
Lubin beneficiation plant	Kombinat Gorniczo Hutniczy Miedzi (KGHM) Polska Miedź S.A. [KGHM, S.A.]
Lubin Mine	Kombinat Gorniczo Hutniczy Miedzi (KGHM) Polska Miedź S.A. [KGHM, S.A.]
Luilu, Kolwezi area	Gécamines
Luisha Mine, Kakanda and Kambove-Likasi area	Gécamines
Luiswishi Mine near Lubumbashi	OMGI (55%), EGMF (25%), and Gecamines (25%) joint venture
Madneuli complex	
Madziwa	Trojan Nickel Mines (Bindura Nickel Corp.)
Malanjkhand Copper Complex mines	Hindustan Copper Co. Ltd.
Maleevsky Mine	Kazzinc JSC
Mantos Blancos open pit mine, SX-EW plant, Region II	Empresa Minera de Mantos Blancos S.A. (Anglo-American plc: 99.9%, other private: 0.1%)
Mantoverde open pit mine, SX-EW plant, Region III	Empresa Minera de Mantos Blancos S.A. (Anglo-American plc: 99.9%, other private: 0.1%)

fac_name	op_comp
Manuel Antonio Matta Plant, Paipote; Osvaldo Martínez Plant, El Salado; Vallenar Plant, Region III; and José Antonio Moreno Plant, Taltal, Regio	Empresa Nacional de Minería (government: 100%)
Maranda	Maranda Mining Co.
Matchless	Ongopolo Mining Ltd.
Miduk copper mine	National Iranian Copper Industries Co. (Government)
Mhangura	Mhangura Copper Mines
Michilla Mine and SX-EW and sulfide leaching plant, 1,500 km north of Santiago	Minera Michilla S.A. (Antofagasta plc: 74.2%, other private Chilean investor: 25.8%)
Mill "Jama" at Bor	Rudarsko Topionicki Bazen Bor (RTB Bor)
Mill at Majdanpek	Rudarsko Topionicki Bazen Bor (RTB Bor)
Mill at Veliki Krivelj	Rudarsko Topionicki Bazen Bor (RTB Bor)
Mine "Jama" at Bor	Rudarsko Topionicki Bazen Bor (RTB Bor)
Mine and mill at Bucim, near Radoviš	Solway Management
Mine and smelter at Cananea, Sonora	Mexicana de Cananea, S.A. de C.V. (Grupo México, S.A. de C.V.: 90%)
Mine at Artemyevskoe	Kazakhmys PLC Mines
Mine at Aitik	Boliden Mineral AB
Mine at Arientero	Atlantic Copper S.A.
Mine at Baia Mare	Compania Nationala REMIN S.A. and Compania Nationala Minvest
Mine at Baia Sprie	Compania Nationala REMIN S.A. and Compania Nationala Minvest
Mine at Bulgan Province	Erdenet Mining Corp. (Mongolian-Russia joint venture)
Mine at Burgas	Rosen
Mine at Burgas	Burgaskii Mines Ltd., Zidorovo
Mine at Chelopech	Chelopech Mining Ltd
Mine at Ertsberg	PT Freeport Indonesia Co.
Mine at Fushë-Arrëz	
Mine at Garpenberg	Boliden Mineral AB

fac_name	op_comp
Mine at Gjegjan	
Mine at Golaj (including Nikoliq and Pus)	
Mine at Grasberg	PT Freeport Indonesia Co.
Mine at Hyesan	Hyesan Youth Copper Mine
Mine at Kankberg	Boliden Mineral AB
Mine at Kristineberg	Boliden Mineral AB
Mine at Kurbnesh-Perlat	
Mine at Långdal	Boliden Mineral AB
Mine at Majdanpek	Rudarsko Topionicki Bazen Bor (RTB Bor)
Mine at Malko Tarnovo	Bradtze
Mine at Narvik	Nikkel og Olivin A/S
Mine at Pahtohavare	Outokumpu Oyj
Mine at Panagyurishte	Asarel-Medet AD.
Mine at Petiknäs	Boliden Mineral AB
Mine at Pirdop	Cumerio Med SA (Pirdop)
Mine at Pirdop	Cumerio Med SA (Pirdop)
Mine at Pyhäsalmi	Inmet Mining Corp.
Mine at Rehovë	
Mine at Renstrom	Boliden Mineral AB
Mine at Reps (including Gurch, Lajo, Spac, and Thurr)	
Mine at Rrëshen	
Mine at Saattopora	Inmet Mining Corp.
Mine at Sepon	Lane Xang Minerals Ltd. (LXML) (wholly owned subsidiary of Oxiana Ltd.)
Mine at Shatyrkul	Kazakhmys PLC Mines
Mine at Shkodër (including Palaj, Karma I and II)	
Mine at Sin Quyen	Lao Cai Copper Complex (wholly owned subsidiary of Vietnam National Minerals Corp.)
Mine at Srednogorie	Elatzite-Med Ltd.
Mine at Srednogorie	Tsar Asen
Mine at Sumbawa Island	PT Newmont Nusa Tenggara
Mine at Veliki Krivelj	Rudarsko Topionički Bazen Bor (RTB Bor)

fac_name	op_comp
Montcalm Mine, 70 km west of Timmins, Ontario	Falconbridge Limited (Noranda Inc.: 58.9%, Falconbridge Limited: 41.1%)
Monywa Copper Project - the Monywa Refinery	Mining Enterprise No.1
Monywa Copper Project - the S&K Mine	Mining Enterprise No.1
Mount Gordon open pit copper (SW-EX) mine (Mammoth)	Aditya Birla Minerals Ltd.
Mount Isa copper smelter	Xstrata plc
Mount Isa underground copper-lead-zinc-silver mine (also includes Enterprise, George Fisher and Hilton mines)	Xstrata plc
Mount Lyell underground copper-gold mine	Sterlite Industries (India) Ltd.
Mount Polley Mine, British Columbia	Imperial Metals Corporation
Mufulira	Mopani Copper Mines plc (Glencore Intl. 73%)
Mufulira	Mopani Copper Mines plc (Glencore Intl. 73%)
Mufulira	Mopani Copper Mines plc (Glencore Intl. 73%)
Muliashi North	ZCCM-IH
Murgul near Artvin	Karadeniz Bakir Isletmeleri A.S. (Etibank, 99.97%)
Murgul, Damar	Karadeniz Bakir Isletmeleri A.S. (Etibank, 99.97%)
Murgul, Smelter	Karadeniz Bakir Isletmeleri A.S. (Etibank, 99.97%)
Myra Falls Mine, British Columbia	Boliden Westmin (Canada) Limited
Nampundwe (Zvishavane Shabanie)	Konkola Copper Mines plc (Anglo American, 65%)
Nchanga	Konkola Copper Mines plc (Anglo American)
Nchanga	Konkola Copper Mines plc (Anglo American, 65%)
Nchanga	Konkola Copper Mines plc (Anglo American, 65%)
Neves Corvo Mine near Castro Verde	Lundin Mining Corp. (LMC)

fac_name	op_comp
Nifty open pit copper (SX-EX) mine	Aditya Birla Minerals Ltd.
Nigramoep & O'okiep	Metorex (Pty) Ltd.
Nigramoep & O'okiep	Metorex (Pty) Ltd.
Nkana	Mopani Copper Mines plc (Glencore Intl, First Quantum)
Nkana	Mopani Copper Mines plc (Glencore Intl, First Quantum)
Nkana	Konkola Copper Mines plc (Anglo American)
Nkana	Smelter Co; Zambia Consolidated Copper Mine-Investments Holdings, plc
Nkana	Zambia Consolidated Copper Mines Ltd. (ZCCM)
Northparkes open pit/underground copper-gold mine	Rio Tinto Ltd.
Noud Mine	Compania Nationala REMIN S.A. and Compania Nationala Minvest
Ok Tedi open pit mine	Ok Tedi Mining Ltd., operator
Ok Tedi open pit mine	Ok Tedi Mining Ltd., operator
Olympic Dam copper smelter	Olympic Dam Operations Pty. Ltd.
Olympic Dam underground copper-silver-gold-uranium mine	Olympic Dam Operations Pty. Ltd.
Open-pit mine, concentrator plant, SX-EW plant, at Ujina, Region I	Compañia Minera Doña Inés de Collahuasi SCM (Anglo-American plc: 44%, Xstrata: 44%, companies led by Mitsui & Co. Ltd.: 12%)
Osborne underground copper-gold mine	Barrick Gold Corp.
Otjihase	Ongopolo Mining Ltd.
Outokumpu flash smelter and electrolytic refinery	Cuprom S.A. Baia Mare
Padcal Copper Project	Philex Mining Corp.
Palabora	Palabora Mining Co. Ltd. (Rio Tinto)
Palabora	Palabora Mining Co. Ltd. (Rio Tinto)
Palabora	Palabora Mining Co. Ltd. (Rio Tinto)
Peak underground gold-zinc-lead-copper-silver underground mine	GoldCorp Inc

fac_name	op_comp
Phoenix	Tati Nickel Mining Co. (Proprietary) Ltd. (LionOre Mining International Ltd., 85%)
Planned Phase 1 mine at Tenke-Fungurume, Likasi area	Tenke Mining Corp.(60%) and Gecamines (40%) joint venture.
Plant at Arientero	Atlantic Copper S.A.
Plant at Baiyin	Baiyin Nonferrous Metals Co.
Plant at Chagai	Saindak Metals Ltd.
Plant at Chanhang	LS-Nikko Copper Inc.
Plant at Chelopech	Chelopech Mining Ltd
Plant at Chifeng	Chifeng Jingeng Copper Co. Ltd.
Plant at Daye	Daye Nonferrous Metals Co.
Plant at Dongying	Dongying Fangyuan Nonferrous Metals Co. Ltd.
Plant at Gresik	PT Smelting Co.
Plant at Guixi	Guixi Smelter
Plant at Huludao	Dongfang Copper Co.
Plant at Jinchuan	Jinchuan Nonferrous Metals Corp.
Plant at Kunming	Yunnan Smelter
Plant at Linyi	Shandong Jinsheng Nonferrous Metals Corp.
Plant at Luoyang	Luoyang Copper Processing Factory
Plant at Malko Tarnovo	Bradtze
Plant at Panagyurishte	Asarel-Medet AD.
Plant at Pirdop	Cumerio Med SA (Pirdop)
Plant at Pirdop	Cumerio Med SA (Pirdop)
Plant at Srednogorie	Elatzite-Med Ltd.
Plant at Srednogorie	Tsar Asen
Plant at Taiyuan	Taiyuan Copper Industry Co.
Plant at Tongling	Jinchang Smelter
Plant at Tongling	Jinchang Smelter
Plant at Wuhu	Wuhu Smelter
Plant at Yanggu	Shandong Yanggu Xiangguang Co. Ltd.
Plant at Yantai	Yantai Penghui Copper Industry Co. Ltd.
Plant at Yuangu	Zhongtiaoshan Nonferrous Metals Co.
Plant at Zhangjiagang	Zhangjiagang United Copper Co.

fac_name	op_comp
Plant in Krompachy	Kovohuty A.S.
Plant in Tianjin	Tianjin Datong Copper Co. Ltd. (former Tianjin Copper Electrolysis Factory)
Polkowice beneficiation plant	(Kombinat Górniczo-Hutniczy Miedzi)(KGHM) Polska Miedz S.A. [KGHM, S.A.]
Polkowice- Sieroszowice Mine	(Kombinat Górniczo-Hutniczy Miedzi)(KGHM) Polska Miedz S.A. [KGHM, S.A.]
Port Kembla copper refinery	Furukawa Co. Ltd.
Potrerillos (Salvador Division)	Corporación Nacional del Cobre de Chile (CODELCO) (government: 100%)
Potrerillos (Salvador Division)	Corporación Nacional del Cobre de Chile (CODELCO) (government: 100%)
Potrerillas SX-EW plants (Salvador Division) (oxide and sulfide)	Corporación Nacional del Cobre de Chile (CODELCO) (government: 100%)
Primary smelter and refinery and secondary plant at Hamburg	Norddeutsche Affinerie AG
Qal`eh Zari Mine, near Birjan	National Iranian Copper Industries Co. (Government)
Quebrada Blanca open-pit mine, Region I	Compañia Minera Quebrada Blanca (Aur Resources Inc.: 76.5%, Inversiones Mineras S.A.: 13.5%)
Raglan Mine in Ungave, Québec	Falconbridge Limited (Noranda Inc.: 58.9%, Falconbridge Limited: 41.1%)
Rapu-Rapu Mine under the Rapu-Rapu polymetallic project	Lafayette Mining, Ltd.
Refinery at Besshi/Toyo (Saijo)	Sumitomo Metal Mining Co. Ltd.
Refinery at Fornaci di Barga	Europametalli - LMI S.p.A.
Refinery at Glogow I	Kombinat Gorniczo Hutniczy Miedzi (KGHM) Polska Miedz S.A. [KGHM, S.A.]
Refinery at Glogow II	Kombinat Gorniczo Hutniczy Miedzi (KGHM) Polska Miedz S.A. [KGHM, S.A.]
Refinery at Gurtnellen	Schmelzmetall AG

fac_name	op_comp
Refinery at Hitachi	Nippon Mining and Metals Co. Ltd. (wholly owned subsidiary of Nikko Kyodo Co. Ltd.)
Refinery at Huelva	Atlantic Copper S.A.
Refinery at Ilo, Moquegua Department	Southern Peru Copper Corp. (SPCC) (Grupo Mexico, S.A. de C.V.: 54.2%, Marmon Corp.: 14.2%, Phelps Dodge Overseas Capital Corp.: 14%, others: 17.6%)
Refinery at Isabel	Philippine Associated Smelting and Refining Corp. (PASAR)
Refinery at Kosaka	Kosaka Smelting and Refining Co. Ltd. (wholly owned subsidiary of Dowa Mining Co. Ltd.)
Refinery at La Oroya, Junin Department	Doe Run Resources Corp. (private: 100%)
Refinery at Legnica	Kombinat Gorniczo Hutniczy Miedzi (KGHM) Polska Miedz S.A. [KGHM, S.A.]
Refinery at Naoshima	Mitsubishi Materials Corp.
Refinery at Niihama	Sumitomo Metal Mining Co. Ltd.
Refinery at Olen	NV Umicore SA
Refinery at Onahama	Onahama Smelting and Refining Co. Ltd.
Refinery at Pieve Vergonte	Sitindustrie S.p.A.
Refinery at Pori	Outokumpu Oyj
Refinery at Porto Marghera	KME Group S.p.A.
Refinery at Rayong	Thai Copper Industries Plc
Refinery at Saganoseki	Nippon Mining and Metals Co. Ltd. (wholly owned subsidiary of Nikko Kyodo Co. Ltd.)
Refinery at Sepon	Lane Xang Minerals Ltd. (LXML) (wholly owned subsidiary of Oxiana Ltd.)
Refinery at Tamano	Hibi Kyodo Smelting Co. Ltd.
Refinery at Tang Loong Commune	Tang Loong Lao Cai Copper Smelting Enterprise (wholly owned subsidiary of Vietnam National Minerals Corp.)
Refinery in Sudbury, Ontario	Inco Limited
Refinery, Sar Cheshmeh copper complex	National Iranian Copper Industries Co. (Government)

fac_name	op_comp
Ridder-Sokolny Mine	Kazzinc JSC
Ridgeway underground gold-copper mine	Newcrest Mining Ltd.
Rolling mill (billet), Sar Cheshmeh copper complex	National Iranian Copper Industries Co. (Government)
Rolling mill (slab), Sar Cheshmeh copper complex	National Iranian Copper Industries Co. (Government)
Rosebery underground zinc-lead-silver-copper-gold mine	OZ Minerals Ltd.
Rosh Pinah	Rosh Pinah Zinc Corp. (Pty.) Ltd.
Rosia Montana Mine	Compania Nationala REMIN S.A. and Compania Nationala Minvest
Roşia Poieni Mine	Compania Nationala REMIN S.A. and Compania Nationala Minvest
Ruashi-Etoile Phase 1, Lubumbashi	Ruashi Mining [Metorex Ltd.of South Africa, Sentinelle Global Investments (Proprietary) Limited and Gecamines]
Ruashi-Etoile Phase 2, Lubumbashi	Ruashi Mining [Metorex Ltd.of South Africa, Sentinelle Global Investments (Proprietary) Limited and Gecamines]
Rudna beneficiation plant	Kombinat Górniczo-Hutniczy Miedzi (KGHM) Polska Miedz S.A. [KGHM, S.A.]
Rudna Mine	Kombinat Górniczo-Hutniczy Miedzi (KGHM) Polska Miedz S.A. [KGHM, S.A.]
Salvador Mining Division, including Inca, Campamento Antiguo, and Damiana Norte Mines - (general coordinates of Chile)	Corporación Nacional del Cobre de Chile (CODELCO) (government: 100%)
Samsun, Smelter and acid plant	Karadeniz Bakır İşletmeleri A.S. (Etibank, 99.97%)
San Cristóbal, Mahr Túnel, and Andaychagua, Junín Department	Cía. Minera Volcán S.A. (private: 100%)
Sanyati	Zimbabwe Mining & Development Corp.
Sar Cheshmeh Mine, Rafsanjan	National Iranian Copper Industries Co. (Government)
Sayak Complex	Kazakhmys PLC Mines
Secondary plant and refinery at Lünen	Hüttenwerke Kayser AG

fac_name	op_comp
Selebi-Phikwe	BCL Ltd. (Botswana RST Ltd., 85%)
Selous	Makwiro Platinum Mines (Pvt.) Ltd. (Zimplats Holdings Ltd.)
Selwyn underground copper-gold mine	Barrick Gold Corp.
Shangani	Trojan Nickel Mines (Bindura Nickel Corp.)
Shituru at Likasi	Gécamines
Silvassa refinery	Sterlite Industries Ltd.
Smelter and electrolytic refinery at Berango, Vizcaya	Elmet SL
Smelter and refinery at Balkhash	Kazakhmys PLC Mines
Smelter and refinery at Rönnskär	Boliden Metals AB
Smelter and refinery at Zhezkazgan	Kazakhmys PLC Mines
Smelter and refinery near Sohar	Oman Mining Co. LLC
Smelter at Antwerp-Hoboken	NV Umicore SA
Smelter at Asua-Bilbao	Industrias Reunidas de Cobre
Smelter at Beerse	Metallo-Chimique NV
Smelter at Bor	Rudarsko Topionicki Bazen Bor (RTB Bor)
Smelter at Brixlegg	Montanwerke Brixlegg AG
Smelter at Harjavalta	Outokumpu Oyj
Smelter at Ilo, Moquegua Department	Southern Peru Copper Corp. (SPCC) (Grupo Mexico, S.A. de C.V.: 54.2%, Marmon Corp.: 14.2%, Phelps Dodge Overseas Capital Corp.: 14%, others: 17.6%)
Smelter at Isabel	Philippine Associated Smelting and Refining Corp. (PASAR)
Smelter at Kristiansand	Nikkelverk A/S
Smelter at Kukës	
Smelter at La Oroya, Junin Department	Doe Run Resources Corp. (private: 100%)
Smelter at Lac	
Smelter at Onsan	LS-Nikko Copper Inc.
Smelter at Onsan	Korea Zinc Co. Ltd.
Smelter at Poissy, Yvelines	Société Française d'Affinage du Cuivre
Smelter at Rubik	

fac_name	op_comp
Smelter at Ust-Kamenogorsk	Kazzinc JSC
Smelter in Sudbury, Ontario	Inco Limited
Smelter in Thompson, Manitoba	Falconbridge Limited (Noranda Inc.: 58.9%, Falconbridge Limited: 41.1%)
Smelter in Timmins, Ontario	Falconbridge Limited (Noranda Inc.: 58.9%, Falconbridge Limited: 41.1%)
Smelter, Khatunabad	National Iranian Copper Industries Co. (Government)
Smelter, Sar Cheshmeh copper complex	National Iranian Copper Industries Co. (Government)
Sungun copper mine	National Iranian Copper Industries Co. (Government)
Strathcona and Timmins operations in Timmins, Ontario	Falconbridge Limited (Noranda Inc.: 58.9%, Falconbridge Limited: 41.1%)
Sudbury Division, Sudbury, Ontario	Falconbridge Limited (Noranda Inc.: 58.9%, Falconbridge Limited: 41.1%)
Teresa Mine	Lepanto Consolidated Mining Company
Thompson district, Manitoba	Inco Limited
Tintaya Mine, Cusco Department	BHP Tintaya S.A. (private: 100%)
Townsville copper refinery	Xstrata plc
Trojan	Trojan Nickel Mines (Bindura Nickel Corp.)
Tsumeb	Ongopolo Processing (Pty.) Ltd.
Tuticorin Smelter	Sterlite Industries Ltd.
Victoria Mine	Lepanto Consolidated Mining Company
Wire plant at Rasht	Simco
Wire rod plant, Sar Cheshmeh copper complex	National Iranian Copper Industries Co. (Government)
Yanacancha Mine, Junin Department	Cia. Minera Atacocha S.A. (private: 100%)
Yauricocha, Junin Department	Cia. Minera San Ignacio de Morococha S.A. (private: 100%)
Zaldivar open-pit, heap-leach mine, Region II	Compañia Minera Zaldivar (Placer Dome Inc.: 100%)
Zangezur copper-molybdenum complex mining Kadzharan deposit	

fac_name	op_comp
	Kapan mining directorate
	Norilsk Nickel
	Norilsk Nickel
	Uralelectromed
	UGMK, 38%; Bashkortostan State, 38%
	Uralelectromed
	Uralelectromed
	Uralelectromed
	Aleksandrinskaya Mining Co.
	Kola Mining and Metals Co.
	Solnechny Mining Combine
	Russian Copper Company
	Urupsky Mining (UGMK)
	Svyatogor Mining
	Uralgidromed
	Kirovgrad Copper
	Svyatogor Mining
	Verkneuralskaya
	Novosibirsk
	Sorsky Mining
	Sredneuralsk Copper
	Almalyk Mining and Metallurgical Combine
	CJSC Armenian Copper Programme (ACP)
	Pechenganikel
	Kola Mining and Metals Co. (Noril'sk)
	Uralgidromed (Russian Copper Company)
	Uralelectromed (Urals Mining & Metallurgical)
	Norilsk
	Russian Copper Company
	Severonikel
	Russian Copper Company
	Yuzhuralnikel
	Kola Mining and Metals Co.

fac_name	op_comp
	Uralgidromed (Russian Copper Company)
	Norilsk G'-M
	Uralelectromed (Urals Mining & Metallurgical)
	Norilsk G'-M
	Kyshtym (refining), 80%
	Uralelectromed
	Severonikel
	Kirovgradsky JSC
	Uralelectromed
	Russian Copper Company

NOTES

This book incorporates my mother's circuit schematics, government mining data, and open-source mapping software, both my own and others'. I asked ChatGPT to produce the geologic timeline in the footer, by posing this question:

Q: Could you please write for me a detailed timeline of the history of the earth, in reverse chronological order? Beginning with the Holocene, or Age of Man, and ending with an epoch within the Hadean period and the formation of the planet itself. Please include all major occurrences of life, as well as mass extinctions.

As I ask ChatGPT for this litany of eras, my query extends backward through geologic time. Our exchange requires material, planetary things: my body-in-chair, fingers on plastic keys. The browser glows on an LED screen. My computer's hardware contains the atomic timelines of cobalt, silicon, copper, and other matter. Somewhere many miles away, OpenAI's server room whirs and heats.

Q: Tell me—do you see yourself as existing as part of this geological timeline?

A: No, I don't perceive myself as existing within the geological timeline. The timeline provided earlier is a historical overview of Earth's physical and biological evolution. As an artificial intelligence created by OpenAI, I am a product of human ingenuity and technology, existing in the realm of information and computation. My "existence" is not tied to the geological or biological processes outlined in Earth's history. I don't have a physical presence or a place in the timeline of life on Earth. My capabilities are centered around language understanding and generation based on the data I've been trained on.

In her final days, my mother suggested I use ChatGPT to complete this book, so as to spend more time as her caregiver. Some users of generative AI compare its creations to dreams, to automatic writing or spiritual mediums. I am cautious about the romantic dimensions of such analogies. Perhaps there are ways I can use the mainframe to speak to the dead, but I have never once wanted to commune with a text corpus trained on my mother. For me, to use ChatGPT is always to reckon with its materiality, with its origins in Silicon Valley capital.

I ask now of the book: Where do these poems begin in geological time? Their origins are less of a point, less of a singularity:

A: The poem begins on a document file on a MacBook Pro.
It uses an Intel Core Processor. It seems to be made of
only light.

A: The poem begins on the planet: the Adirondack lakes;
the Tucson deserts; the mine in Machalí, Chile; the city of
Providence, Rhode Island on Narragansett land.

A: The poem comes from a summer of Canadian wildfire smoke,
from constant rain and flooding. I wrote the earliest versions
of these poems across a series of artist books: sewn,
typewritten, found leaf transferred in charcoal onto paper.

A: The poem always comes from the body.

A: The poem emerges. It comes from a cacophonous space:
a billion people talking, all at once—

Benton-Cohen, Katherine. *Borderline Americans: Racial Division and Labor War in the Arizona Borderlands*. Cambridge: Harvard University Press, 2011.

Crawford, Kate, and Trevor Paglen. "Excavating AI: The Politics of Images in Machine Learning Training Sets." *AI In Society* 36, no. 3 (2021): 1105–1116.

Crawford, Kate. *Atlas of AI: Power, Politics, and the Planetary Costs of Artificial Intelligence*. New Haven: Yale University Press, 2022.

Glissant, Édouard. *Poetics of Relation*. Translated by Betsy Wing. Ann Arbor: University of Michigan Press, 1997.

Hawley, Charles Caldwell. *A Kennecott Story: Three Mines, Four Men, and One Hundred Years, 1887–1997*. Salt Lake City: University of Utah Press, 2014.

Hu, Tung-Hui. *A Prehistory of the Cloud*. Cambridge: MIT Press, 2016.

Kim, Eunsong. "Found, Found, Found, Lived, Lived, Lived: The Archival Labor of Carrie Mae Weems and Sasha Huber." *Scapegoat Journal 9* (2016).

Mattern, Shannon. "Cloud and Field: On the Resurgence of 'Field Guides' in a Networked Age." *Places Journal*, August 1, 2016.

Nakamura, Lisa. "Indigenous Circuits: Navajo Women and the Racialization of Early Electronic Manufacture." *American Quarterly* 66, no. 4 (2014): 919–41.

Nowak, Mark, with Ian Teh. *Coal Mountain Elementary: New and Selected Poems*. Minneapolis: Coffee House Press, 2009.

O'Gieblyn, Meghan. "Babel." *n+1*, September 29, 2021.

Oliveros, Pauline. *Deep Listening: A Composer's Sound Practice*. Bloomington: iUniverse, Inc., 2005.

Ono, Yoko. *Grapefruit*. New York: Simon and Schuster, 1971.

Parikka, Jussi. *A Geology of Media*. Minneapolis: University of Minnesota Press, 2015.

Redniss, Lauren. *Oak Flat: A Fight for Sacred Land in the American West*. New York: Random House, 2021.

Rukeyser, Muriel. *The Book of the Dead*. Morgantown: West Virginia University Press, 2018.

Vogt, Naomi. "Small Monuments: Recording and Forgetting in the Work of Steve McQueen." *Third Text* 29, no. 3 (2015): 123–40.

Yusoff, Kathryn. *A Billion Black Anthropocenes or None*. Minneapolis: University of Minnesota Press.

ACKNOWLEDGMENTS

Thank you, Corinne Butta and Rachel Valinsky, for bringing this project into the world with such care, and to Bhanu Kapil, for seeing something here. To Corinne especially, for our editorial conversations. To Dorothy Lin for the detailed tasks of book design, typesetting, and giving it all shape.

Thank you to *Tupelo Quarterly*, *Nat Brut*, and Tilted House Press for publishing earlier versions of select poems.

Beloved friends of the MFA: Min, Jackson, Jana, Kate, Brian K., Tiffany, Allison, Sophia, Chloe, Riley. I'm grateful to the Blue Mountain Center—most of all Romy, Merry and staff, whose labor made it possible to write and feel more patiently. Cari, Laura, Victoria, Jung Sun, Dulani, for pants, tarot, and strawberry abundance.

To Sawako Nakayasu and John Cayley—I'm grateful for your advisership and expansive ethos. To Eleni Sikelianos for ways of listening; Jennifer Elise Foerster for encouragement on early drafts; Maralie Armstrong-Rial for perspectives on the cloud.

LA Warman encouraged dirt into the mouth—she articulated dental envy first. In Louisville, Makalani Bandele shared his original concept of circuit-as-poem.

To Laurie McKenna for Bisbee conversations; Mairéad Byrne and Rick Benjamin for supporting my writing over the years.

The poem "A FRAGMENTED LINEAR ACCOUNT" uses paraphrased and direct language by Dionne Brand and Eunsong Kim. I'm thankful to be writing with the influence of their work. "This cannot be the ending, yes?" is from Eunsong Kim's description of her poem "Romance #1." I remember the phrase "They hate birds" from

Dionne Brand's reading and comments at Brown University in 2023. "Endless names of stones" is from a poem in Brand's *In Another Place, Not Here*. Kathryn Yusoff writes about this in *A Billion Black Anthropocenes or None*.

Emphatically: Thank you, thank you to Kimberly Alidio, Bhanu Kapil, and Allison Parrish for writing about this book with such care.

Friends, for your loving presence in artmaking and grief: Celine, Hua, Katy G., Hanna E., Nathier, Ying, Erin K., Nonto, Taka, Lily X., Ryan G., Minsoo, Tim, Phillip, Karishma, Basalt. To Aarón for vegan completos and our trip to El Teniente. To Willy with love.

Jonathan: for confluence, for grounding me and this project through all weathers.

To Ma, an ancestor now, whose love remains and exceeds.

She Will Last as Long as Stones
© 2025 kathy wu

All rights reserved. No part of this book may be used or reproduced without prior permission of the publisher.

Passage Series #12
First Edition, 2025
Edition of 1,000 copies
ISBN: 979-8-9909878-8-3
LCCN: 2025942746

Edited by Corinne Butta
Proofread by Juwon Jun
Designed by Dorothy Lin
Typeset in FT 88 and Hershey, a typeface originally drawn by Dr. Allen Vincent Hershey in 1967 and revived by Bryant Wells in 2019
Printed at Balto, Lithuania

Distributed in the USA by Asterism Books
asterismbooks.com

Distributed in Europe/the UK by Antenne Books
antennebooks.com

The authorized representative in the EU for product safety and compliance is eucomply OÜ, Pärnu mnt 139b-14, 11317 Tallinn, Estonia, hello@eucompliancepartner.com, +33757690241.
Our official distribution partner is Antenne books, ltd.

Published by Wendy's Subway
379 Bushwick Avenue
Brooklyn, NY 11206
wendyssubway.com

Wendy's Subway is a non-profit reading room, writing space, and independent publisher located in Brooklyn.

The Passage Series features titles by emerging writers and artists whose work manifests in innovative, hybrid, and cross-genre forms that imagine new possibilities and expressions of the poetic, the political, and the social.

She Will Last as Long as Stones is the 2024 Open Reading Period awardee, selected by guest judge Bhanu Kapil.

The Passage Series is supported, in part, by the New York State Council on the Arts with support of the Office of the Governor and the New York State Legislature, and public funds from the New York City Department of Cultural Affairs in Partnership with the City Council.